LIVING PRESENCE

Other publications compiled and translated by
Kabir Helminski

The Ruins of the Heart: Selected Lyric Poetry of Jelaluddin Rumi
The Drop that Became the Sea: Selected Lyric
Poetry of Yunus Emre

With Camille Helminski

Rumi: Daylight. A Daybook of Spiritual Guidance
Happiness Without Death: Desert Hymns of Assad Ali

LIVING PRESENCE

*A Sufi Way to
Mindfulness
and the Essential Self*

KABIR EDMUND HELMINSKI

JEREMY P. TARCHER/PERIGEE

Jeremy P. Tarcher/Perigee Books
are published by
The Putnam Publishing Group
200 Madison Avenue
New York, NY 10016
First Jeremy P. Tarcher/Perigee Edition 1992

Library of Congress Cataloging-in-Publication Data

Helminski, Kabir, date.
  Living presence : a Sufi way to mindfulness and the essential self /
Kabir Edmund Helminski.
    p.   cm.
  ISBN 0-87477-699-6 : $9.95
  1. Sufism—Prayer-books and devotions—English.   I. Title.
BP189.62.H45   1992   92-4974
297 ' .43—dc20   CIP

Design by Mauna Eichner

Printed in the United States of America
  2   3   4   5   6   7   8   9   10
This book is printed on acid-free paper.

Contents

Acknowledgments

In my spiritual search I owe a great debt to so many people who have been guiding lights: for my early education the Jesuits, especially Martin D'Arcy, S.J.; Shibayama Roshi and Suzuki Roshi, the first Zen masters I ever met; Murshid Samuel Lewis and Ram Das with whom I lived and worked at the Lama Foundation; various students of Gurdjieff, especially William Segal and Pierre Elliot; Reshad Feild for his insights and friendship; Shaikh Suleyman Dede for his immense good will, who guided us on the way of Mevlana Jelaluddin Rumi; Celalettin Chelebi for his support and guidance; Hasan Shushud for the sweetness of annihilation; Shaikh Tosun Bayrak al-Jerrahi for his steady support; Murat Yagan for his unique clarity and profoundly positive effect on my thinking; Ilhami Baba, Turgut Koca, Oruc Guvenc, Metin, Ihsan, Hasan Dede, and Muhittin Baba for their spiritual hospitality and conversation; Refik Algan for his invaluable friendship and guidance; Dr. Abdul Aziz Said for networking at the highest levels; and Dr. Assad Ali for what no words can express.

Acknowledgments are also due to these people: my wife Camille for her spiritual companionship over more than seventeen years; Thomas Goldberg for his editorial suggestions; David and Marion McClelland who offered their Maui home, which became the setting in which this book came to completion; Jeremy Tarcher, who generously demonstrated his appreciation of these ideas; and the very cordial and professional people at Jeremy P. Tarcher, Inc.

Presence:
An Introduction

A common theme runs through all the great spiritual traditions. It goes by many names—awakening, recollection, mindfulness, *dhyana*, remembrance, *zhikr*, presence—and by no name at all. This state of consciousness adds further dimensions to being in this world. Beyond the narrow band of awareness that has come to be accepted as the conventional state of consciousness is a faculty that is the master key to unlocking our latent human potential.

In certain teachings, such as Buddhism, the practice of mindful presence is the central fact. In Islam remembrance is the qualifier of all activity. In Christianity we must look to the experience of its great mystics and to prayer of the heart. But in all authentic spiritual psychologies this state of consciousness is a fundamental experience and requirement. For the purposes of our reflections I shall call it *presence*.

Presence signifies the quality of *consciously being here*. It is the activation of a higher level of awareness that allows all our other human functions—such as thought, feeling, and action—to be known, developed, and harmonized. Presence is the way in which we occupy space, as well as how we flow and move. Presence shapes our self-image and emotional tone. Presence determines the degree of our alertness, openness, and warmth. Presence decides whether we leak and scatter our energy or embody and direct it.

Presence is the human self-awareness that is the end result of the evolution of life on this planet. Human presence is not merely quantitatively different from other forms of life; humanity represents a new form of life, of concentrated spiritual energy sufficient to produce will. With will, the power of conscious choice, human beings can formulate intentions, transcend their instincts and desires, educate themselves, and steward the natural world. Unfortunately, humans can also use this power to exploit nature and tyrannize other human beings. This potency of will, which on the one hand can connect us to conscious harmony, can also lead us in the direction of separation from that same harmony.

I have been speaking of presense as a human attribute, with the understanding that it is the presence of Absolute Being reflected through the human being. We can learn to activate this presence at will. Once activated, this presence can be found both within and without. Because we find it extending beyond the boundaries of what we thought was ourselves, we are freed from separation, from duality. We can then speak of being *in* this presence.

Many people today live in a pluralist, postmodern, postreligious age. Few people have the security of being true believers in anything. We live at a time when the stories, belief systems, and mythologies of past centuries have lost their credibility and yet are more available to all of us than ever before in human history. We see them as relative truths now, not absolutes. The margins of cultures have become porous; parochialism is dissolving, but we do not yet have a shared spiritual vocabulary. Yet the world is moving toward an unprecedented economic, psychological, and spiritual convergence. We are so many people, sharing a limited space. Communication is becoming universal and instantaneous.

Humankind needs a spiritual philosophy that is equal to this explosion of technology and communication. We need a feeling for the nobility and responsibility of being human, as we need an awareness of the unity of all life, or we will succumb to unconscious forces that will drag us down. Perhaps more than ever before, we need a way to activate and develop our latent humanity to balance the forces that challenge it—the unprecedented means of satisfying our desires and the prevailing ignorance about the meaning and purpose of life.

But we needn't be pessimistic; the creative power at the heart of life will ultimately discover its own most appropriate expression.

I would like to share in the most universal terms some of the experiences, reflections, and knowledge that I have met in my encounter with some sources of traditional wisdom. It is time that these ideas entered into the very heart of our culture. Presented in universal terms, they may pass through the walls of resistance that some of our cultural and religious conditioning has set up.

I owe much to the living teachers who have generously shared their knowledge and their presence. I have referred to various teachers as "my teacher" in this book because I wished to stress their functional role rather than their biographical identity.

Different people within the broad tradition of love and presence have given me what I could receive and what they could give. Without this living connection, I would not have begun to grasp the teachings left by various traditions. What I owe to the spiritual history of mankind is implicit in all that I will have to say here.

Much of my adult life has been occupied with an inquiry into various spiritual psychologies and practices. I have traveled the path, and I have explored some side roads and dead ends. For about twenty years I have been involved in an experiment of applying the traditional wisdom of the East and Middle East in a North American environment. My own experience has proven to me that the practice of presence is an essential means to live a fully human life here and now and to know those qualities that are described as spiritual.

This presence is like a passport to greater life. Presence is our connection to that greater Being to which we belong, but which is often buried beneath mundane concerns, bodily desires, emotional disturbances, and mental distractions. Through knowledge, practice, and understanding, this presence can be awakened. Eventually, we will not be without it—whether in speaking or moving, whether in thinking or feeling. Awakening this presence is the most reliable and direct means of cultivating our essential human qualities, of activating everything that we need to meet the conditions of our lives. Presence is the point of intersection between the world of the senses and the world of the Spirit. May we never cease to discover its beauty and power.

This book is meant to offer certain transformative ideas that carry an energy of their own. But it is necessary to apply these ideas, to live these teachings. The application of these ideas must be left for you to discover; otherwise you will not have the right kind of relationship with this knowledge. In the following pages I offer some suggestions for ways of practicing these ideas, but I do not mean for these to be taken as final or complete. In order to make these ideas your own, it is necessary to be both receptive to their force and active in applying them in your life.

I have tried to achieve some clarity and consistency of language regarding a subject that can be elusive. I apologize for whatever confusion or other shortcomings you may find.

Kabir Helminski
Ulupalakua, Maui, Hawaii, 1991

The Master said: There is one thing in this world which must never be forgotten. If you were to forget everything else, but did not forget that, then there would be no cause to worry; whereas if you performed and remembered and did not forget every single thing, but forgot that one thing, then you would have done nothing whatsoever. It is just as if a king had sent you to a country to carry out a specified task. You go and perform a hundred other tasks; but if you have not performed that particular task on account of which you had gone to the country, it is as though you have performed nothing at all. So man has come into this world for a particular task, and that is his purpose; if he does not perform it, then he will have done nothing.

DISCOURSES OF RUMI (TRANSLATED BY A. J. ARBERRY)

The City of Separation: A Tale of Transformation

There was once a city covered by clouds. In it were great office buildings, schools, stores, and factories. The city was a place where raw materials, both physical and human, flowed. It was the center of the economy. It was where you *had* to be to be an important, successful person, but it was also a place where many terrible things happened. The majority of people in their own estimation were failures; no person or place was secure from various unlawful acts; and the conditions supported in this environment produced an infinite variety of illnesses, including some that were deadly and contagious.

This city was very dark. Energy had become quite limited and little light was available. People passed one another in shadows and could not easily see one another. Perhaps to be noticed more, they improvised various extreme forms of behavior and dress.

In this place it was typical for people to live in fear and suspicion. Even so-called friends withheld much from one another. If you asked who was in charge, you would be told, "We are all free here; we follow our own selves. No one controls us. This is just the way things are."

At first I had found this city interesting. I was drawn to walking its dark streets at all hours. I wished to be an observer, but increasingly I was becoming more a part of it. Eventually I began to wish to find some other life, or change something inside myself, but as often as I thought about it, nothing ever changed. I once asked someone, "Am I the only one who feels that something is not right? Or do others sometimes feel this way?"

"Sure, we all complain," he answered. "But this is life. We have to adjust to reality. Why whistle in the wind? But there is a neighborhood of this city where you can find people who feel the way you do."

I was informed of the neighborhood of Remorse, as it was called, and came to know the people there. They were in every respect like the other people of this city, except that they felt remorse over some of their actions. Among the population were many arrogant, envious, and insincere individuals who took pleasure in getting the upper hand in every situation. I came to know them well—their selfishness and doubt, their obsessions and hesitations, their remorse, and their inevitable acceptance of their weakness.

I asked, "Why don't people change? Why do they only think about it and never do it? Why don't we consider how all this will end?"

By some chance a few of the people of this neighborhood found their way out of the city and came to the village of Sharing. They found it either through real desperation or by accident. A sign at the village limits says, "Spirit in us All." This village was the home of Ms. Affection. The people here enjoyed many forms of togetherness. They had many occasions for celebration, and they sang songs together and danced. Their children were respected and allowed plenty of play time, and they were also given useful work. Travelers were always welcomed and cared for. Family members did not fear getting old and useless. When one of them might fall sick, others took this as a special opportunity to visit. Married people did not fear judgment or abandonment.

Lovers were guiltless and pure. Each person valued his or her work because of how it fit into the whole, and everyone had something to work at because all were needed by the others.

But more than anything, what kept the people happy was the totally irrational and immeasurable love they felt for their Ms. Affection. Once people had met her there was little chance of their ever returning to the city.

Unlike the people of that city, who acted solely and predictably from their own self-interest, these people of Sharing were unpredictable. They acted irrationally, giving away the best they had and expecting nothing in return. These people lived in a mist of love. They would not have survived well in most other places, but here in Sharing one found rich and poor together. The most educated were humbly teaching those who wished to know more. Those who were served respected those who served. I immediately felt relaxed and at home, even joyous. My life went along smoothly for some time before I began to feel something unsettled in my heart. When I saw a certain old man whose face was radiant with life and compassion, I told him, "Maybe you can help me. I cannot seem to remember what it is I really want."

"What do you deeply love?"

"When I was in the city I had forgotten about love. When I came to this village, I realized that there was nothing I wanted more than to be here with these people, but now I am not sure."

"Beyond this village, my son, is a place you might visit," he said. "Don't worry, I can easily take you there. In this place, you may meet, God willing, four kinds of people:

"First, there are the Pretenders. You will see them reading and talking about the Truth, even doing the postures of meditation and the forms of worship, but their minds are often somewhere else. And yet they are practicing the ways of love, the fruits of love, as if they really knew love, and this will save them in the end. They are learning that the One has many names. May their imitation become reality.

3

"Then there are the Warriors. They practice the Greater Work, the struggle with the ego. They are quiet and gentle, thankful and courteous. The activities they love are the simple acts of living, prayer, and spontaneous service. They have shed the artificialities of the ego and its many distractions. Their egos have been tamed by love, found submission, and learned to serve their great Self. If you find them, stay with them long enough to learn patience and the real contentment.

"Third, you may meet, God willing, the People of Remembrance. They remember the One inwardly in all they do. They eat little, sleep little, and speak little lest they distract one another's attention from the presence of the One. They are the easiest people to be with—light as feathers, never a burden on anyone. If you spend many years with them, God willing, you might overcome your forgetfulness, doubt, and withholding. But even when you do, you will still have the hidden contradiction of I and He."

At this moment I was overcome with such sadness, and the tears were flowing before I knew it. I wanted to drown in this sea of sorrow, because I felt so far from anything real—so lost—but the sight of the radiant face of my old friend took away my sense of hopelessness.

"Oh dear one," he said, "slave of your own ego, orphan, exile, beggar, the fourth group you will meet, God willing, are the People of Total Submission. They are speechless. They undertake no unnecessary action on their own, but there is no obstacle to the will of their great Self, no hesitation, no second thoughts, no bargaining. They have reached the most subtle state of themselves and know their own nothingness. These people ask nothing for themselves because they are identified with the creative power Itself. You may live among them for many years until you know of their state and your actions appear as theirs, but you will not be inwardly one of them if you still suffer from separation, if you are still yourself, if you still feel lover *and* beloved. If your experience still comes from the well of your own subconscious, by your own inner faculties—as long as a trace of you remains in you—you have not attained your purpose. Know that there is a knowledge and a certainty that comes through Spirit alone. Spirit plus Nothing: that is your highest destiny."

I have updated and retold this story, which is from an unpublished nineteenth-century Sufi source, so that those of us who are searching will reflect on where it is *we* live, and *where we are going.*

Soul Work,
Reflecting Spirit

Abundance is seeking the beggars and the poor,
just as beauty seeks a mirror.
Beggars, then, are the mirrors of God's abundance,
and they that are with God are
united with Absolute Abundance.

RUMI, *MATHNAWI*, I, 2745, 2750

Education as it is currently understood, particularly in the West, ignores the human soul, or essential Self. This essential Self is not some vague entity whose existence is a matter of speculation, but our fundamental "I," which has been covered over by social conditioning and by the superficiality of our rational mind. In North America we are in great need of a form of training that would contribute to the awakening of the essential Self. Such forms of training have existed in other eras and cultures and have been available to those with the yearning to awaken from the sleep of their limited conditioning and know the potential latent in the human being. We are made to know ourselves; we are created for this self-awareness; we are fully equipped for it. What could be more important than to know ourselves?

The education of the soul, or essential Self, is different from the education of the personality or the intellect. Conventional education is all about acquiring external knowledge and becoming something in the outer world. The education of the soul involves not only knowledge, but the realization of a presence that is our deeper nature and that includes attention, will, and self-transcendence.

What is most characteristically human is not guaranteed to us by our species or by our culture but given only in potential. A spiritual master once expressed it this way: A person must work in order to become human.

What is most distinctly human in us is something more than the role we play in society and more than the conditioning, whether for good or bad, of our culture. It is our essential Self, which is our point of contact with infinite Spirit. This Spirit is not to be understood as a metaphysical assertion or belief, but as something we can experience for ourselves.

You, as a human being, are the end product of a process in which this Spirit has evolved better and better reflectors of Itself. If the human being is the most evolved carrier of the Creative Spirit—possessing conscious love, will, and creativity—then our humanity is the degree to which this physical/spiritual vehicle, and particularly our nervous system, can reflect or manifest Spirit. That which is most sacred in us, that which is deeper than our individual personality, is our connection to this Spirit, Cosmic Life, Creative Power, or whatever name we may use.

Whereas conventional religious belief has the tendency to anthropomorphize God/Spirit, this process consists in the "Godization," one might say, of the human being. Our human nature is realized through the understanding and awareness that the essential human Self is a reflection of Spirit. To become truly human is to attain a tangible awareness of Spirit, to realize oneself as a reflection of Spirit, or God.

The Work I hope to describe is a process of awakening a transcending awareness, a presence that can initiate and sustain the activation of our latent human faculties. A certain knowledge, help, and practice is called for in order for us to become human beings, to know what we *are*. A person must have this Work, because many of our human attributes have atrophied. Through disuse they have become latent faculties rather than functioning ones. The human being has not only the faculties of sense, emotion, and intelligence that we already know, but other faculties or senses—volitional, psychic, intuitive, magnetic, and ecological. A purified and energized nervous system with all these faculties functioning harmoniously would lead a person to experience the unity of Being—unity with the Cosmic Life and with the Creative Power.

For this a balanced program for the realization of our latent, essential Self is necessary. This essential Self is not an absolute term but a relative one signifying that purified subjectivity or awareness that we come to know as we become relatively free of the identifications with our social programming and conditioning. This essential Self will be found to have the attributes of Spirit, including unconditional love and fundamental creativity.

Realization, in its fullest meaning, is not merely knowing something, but making it *real* in oneself. We come to this essential Self through a process of deconditioning, reconditioning, and unconditioning. The West offers few traditional models for this kind of intentional human development. Neither in our universities nor in our churches has this work gone on in a systematic way. These institutions have yielded little beyond the development of intellectuality and conventional religious behavior. Occult and initiatic societies in the West, with few exceptions, have offered little more than ceremonialism, intellectualism, and psychic distraction. A culture that ignores this work of awakening our latent humanity will be starved of the food of the soul.

It would be useful to distinguish between the Work, on the one hand, and religion or philosophy, on the other. The Work is an approach to Spirit involving a total commitment and way of life. A religion is a system of beliefs and rituals that may or may not be a form of the Work for any particular person. A philosophy is a system of ideas, an investigation into the principles that underlie knowledge and reality; it is primarily a mental system.

The religiously inclined person may ask, "What should I believe?"; the philosophical person might ask, "What is truth?"; but the one who asks, "How shall I *find* God, how shall I *experience* Spirit, how shall I *become* the Truth?" is asking the questions of the Work. What is sought is sought through experience, through a process of maturing, through using more and more of our faculties, through a gradual change of perception.

Some important spiritual issues of our time are whether or not the Work needs the support of a tradition and to what extent such traditions are viable in the pluralist, postmodern world. Today there is a resistance to religious and traditional language by a great number of intelligent people. This is not necessarily a resistance to the truths religious language formerly expressed, but to the cheapening and conventionalizing of Reality. For Reality, after all, is what we mean by God. When the wonder of this Reality is traded for slogans and self-righteousness, it is not surprising that many turn from religion.

How shall those truths now be understood, expressed, and realized? As various individuals and groups attempt to apply traditional forms of spiritual training, they have to deal with the aspects of those forms that were suited to another time and place. Discriminating between what is essential and what is inappropriate is not a task for amateurs, and it is not a task that many traditionalists will agree is necessary.

It is also necessary for new forms of training to be developed that are appropriate to the ever-changing condition of human beings. Only when the higher levels of realization are grasped is it possible to innovate and adapt the teaching to the new milieu. Tradition, if it is sacred and authentic, is always adapting and innovating. But today's culture faces greater discontinuities than any other in known history, as witnessed by the fact that the total amount of information with which humans must deal is doubling in a matter of years rather than centuries.

Everywhere we see a spiritual hunger that goes unsatisfied, and we also see some rather exotic and bizarre ways of trying to satisfy this hunger. What form might the inner development of human beings take in the world at this time? The West has had some history of spiritual experiments that aimed toward intentional human development. But for the most part even these attempts have been both isolated and experimental, without an adequate traditional knowledge—such as has been more available in the East and Middle East—to sustain and guide them. Today, nearing the end of a century, we have a network of spiritual organizations, some of them selling their ideas and services in the marketplace, others requiring adoption or imitation of foreign cultures, still others attempting to offer wisdom and well-being in convenient weekend workshops.

Many traditional cultures have developed forms of the Work. My own search for understanding began with the systems of the Far East and eventually brought me to the Sufi tradition, particularly as it has been practiced in Asia Minor and Central Asia. What impressed me about this tradition was how well integrated it is with the practical side of life. It seems that those who develop within this tradition attain spiritual maturity without sacrificing their participation in a truly human life. They prove themselves effective in the world, as members of society, as parents, and as lovers.

There is a knowledge and a practice of connecting ourselves

with cosmic Life. It has nothing to do with belief; it is learned. It is increased by our consciousness of it, by our increasing awareness of the abundance of cosmic energy. Life is infinite, and this infinity can be tapped. The only limitation is one of awareness.

Life is not just this bioenergetic vitality, but a spiritual vitality that is eternal, and we are that. This lifespan that we know on earth is said to be one chapter in the story of Life. This Eternal Life reflects through us.

A seed has no energy of its own, but it can come alive in the right environment. Every form of life has a capacity for response but none so much as the human being. In an infertile environment this capacity for response may be dormant. The cultivation we need to provide is through conscious awareness. This makes the difference between nominally being alive and being alive abundantly. With awareness we can develop all our faculties. The body, mind, spirit, and ecology form an interconnected whole. When a harmonious relationship exists among all of these, we have abundant life.

Once a teacher of mine was asked, while having coffee in a diner, what the Work is aiming toward. He wrote these words on the back of a napkin: *"As human beings we can work together in order to 1. develop our nervous system through inner work; 2. develop our physical bodies through conscious exercise, right breathing and eating; 3. develop our sense of interdependence and altruism; 4. develop the priority of common cause; 5. develop in social relations; 6. develop in family and conjugal relations; 7. develop an abundant livelihood through the quality of our work; 8. work for the ecology; 9. develop a grasp of Truth; and attain It in this world."*

The first steps in this process may be intellectual. Our description of spiritual realities and spiritual work is not meant to be absolute, final, or complete. We must never foreget that Reality or Truth is beyond anything we can say, and yet as human beings we will realize ourselves more completely if our ideas are in harmony with our possibilities. It may not be possible or necessary to say what Absolute Truth is, but for the human being the Truth is that we are integral to It, not separate, and can experientially realize this.

It is necessary to attain some intellectual clarity, but once the conscious mind has become familiar with certain transformative ideas, these ideas may penetrate to the level of subconscious mind, which is traditionally called "the heart." Having been received and grasped as far as this level, these ideas help to create a new receptivity of mind to all the levels of Being.

The Work, the practical aspect, is primary; the intellectual expression of this process is necessary, but secondary. The purpose of this formulation is not only to be read by the mind, but to be acted on in a coherent way. Ideas must become values, not mere steps in a logical process. The idea of *presence,* for instance, is a practical one. It is not a belief or opinion, but a practice. When a person has learned it and has practiced it, it becomes grasped and valued.

The four terms diagrammed below represent, in a necessarily simplified way, the fundamental terms and polarities of the Self as presented in this book. All of the terms employed are unfortunately subject to various definitions in the English language,

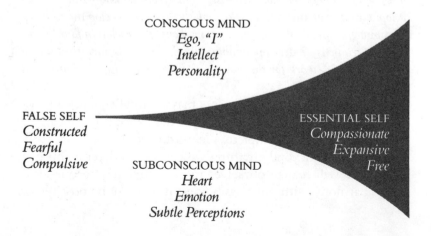

CONSCIOUS MIND
Ego, "I"
Intellect
Personality

FALSE SELF
Constructed
Fearful
Compulsive

ESSENTIAL SELF
Compassionate
Expansive
Free

SUBCONSCIOUS MIND
Heart
Emotion
Subtle Perceptions

and so it is important to clarify at the outset what is meant by them here.

We begin with a sense of self, an "I." Before we say whether this "I" really exists or not, we can say that it is something we all experience. What this experience is like varies enormously from person to person, from a contracted, separate self to an expanded, spiritualized Self. Commonly, however, this "I" is a very small part of ourselves. It is as much of ourselves as we are conscious.

Beyond this "I" or conscious mind is a vast realm that can be called the Subconscious. Commonly, it is viewed as a kind of warehouse of buried memories, conditioning, complexes, drives, and obsessions. From a more spiritual perspective this Subconscious is also the Heart, the source of wisdom and subtle perceptions. It is infinite, at least compared to the conscious mind, and is spontaneously in communication with other minds and Mind-at-large.

The other polarity that needs clarification involves the false self and the essential Self. The basic premise of this book is that the conscious mind is largely identified with the false self, which is the product of fear and selfishness. We can disidentify with this self and through presence realize our identity with the essential Self. Both the terms *false self* and *essential Self* are relative. From the perspective of the essential Self we feel our unity with everything through love and through the finer faculties of mind.

Where we identify ourselves on the false self and essential Self spectrum influences our experience of "I," as well as the condition of our subconscious mind. Clearly, people whose lives are ruled by vanity and all the delusions it brings will have a different sense of self than those who can be aware of their dependence on Spirit and their interdependence with the whole of life, those who are humble and remember the fact of their own death. The former will be enslaved to the tyranny of their own ego; the latter will experience an abundant and creative life, living from the essential Self.

Spiritual attainment is a process of becoming complete by allowing the mind and heart to respond to the highest levels of Spirit. Spiritual maturity is not a process of personal development, because the "person" on whom such development is based is a superficial identity. This is one of the most difficult things to learn. For many years I thought I was "in the Work" to make "me" a conscious person, as if it were an achievement similar to other achievements. Only slowly and painfully did I begin to learn that the real Work is to serve, to pay attention to how other human beings can be helped toward freedom and love by being an example of those qualities without expectation of any recognition or reward.

We are reflectors of this greater Spirit. All intelligence, all beauty, all strength, all compassion, all forgiveness, all patience, and all trust are gifts and attributes of this Spirit. As the awareness of our connection with Spirit increases, these attributes are reflected more perfectly through us. To the extent that we polish the mirror of the heart, we become reflective and bright. We become lovers of this pure Spirit.

How is this Spirit to be found? If it is everywhere, it should not be too difficult to find. But where is it most concentrated?

Firstly, the Spirit is most concentrated in the human heart, when the human turns toward it and realizes it within. By turning toward our own experience, by cultivating a vigilance regarding our own states, we can come to know ourselves and therefore know the Spirit we reflect.

Secondly, wherever two or more are gathered in remembrance, maturity of spirit is communicated from one heart to another. It is rarely achieved alone. For a number of reasons friendship and brotherhood are the outcome of our understanding the Truth.

The group or sister/brotherhood exists to assist in the attraction, concentration, and transmission of subtle energies leading to new perceptions and personal transformation. Many ways have been developed to engender a resonance among human beings. Through conscious worship with a concentration on movement, sound, and breath, certain states are facilitated that open us to the relatively infinite capacities of mind.

Spiritual work has traditionally been founded upon a group model, taking advantage of group dynamics to practice such values as remembrance, service, selflessness, humility, generosity, and community. To approach the work alone is not only a great limitation, but it runs the risk of cultivating self-importance and self-righteousness. Spiritual attainment apart from other human beings is illusory and incomplete. The awakening of latent human qualities while still based on the ego and without the support of love is possible only to a limited extent. The purpose of the Work is not only to awaken our own latent human qualities; it should proceed under the protective grace of humility and affection. The real Work is completed under the protection and guidance of Love.

Our tendency is toward personal independence, but in order to know our real Self we need to abandon the ego-protective behaviors that keep us in separation. We need to open ourselves to other beings in this milieu of Love. We need to gather with the followers of Reality to receive the gift of maturity and to offer ourselves generously. Only as we begin to open to others in love can the isolated ego be transformed. An awareness of our interdependence with our fellow human beings and with all of life provides the environment in which the seed of the soul can flourish.

Creative Energy
and Human Capacities

See how the hand is invisible while the pen is writing;
the horse careening, yet the rider unseen;
the arrow flying, but the bow out of sight;
individual souls existing,
while the Soul of souls is hidden

RUMI, *MATHNAWI*, II, 1303–304

The conventional world view is one of fragmentation rather than wholeness, of separateness rather than unity. We take this fragmentation and meaninglessness as reality. The idea that reality is a whole and we are integral to it—not merely a piece of it—is viewed with some skepticism or, at best, mere intellectual agreement. We fail to experience this unity except in exceptional moments, the significance of which cannot be integrated into everyday life because these moments happen in a very different state of consciousness.

How we perceive the world depends on how we understand it. Our ideas shape our experience of reality, and it is with our ideas of reality that we should begin if we are going to be at home in the world of unity. Ideas alone may not bring us into that unified reality, but those rooted in meaninglessness, disunity, and separation need to be weeded out. Furthermore, ideas that support the experience of unity and presence need to be learned so thoroughly that their significance is transferred to the subconscious mind.

At some point in the history of the modern world, human minds could no longer support the traditional spiritual ideas of a meaningful order and the whole structure supporting Western spiritual belief came crashing down. Perhaps the structure itself did not accord with nature, or perhaps it had deviated too far from reality to be supported any longer. Human beings stand in the rubble of former beliefs. We finger through the shards of meaning, trying to imagine what the whole might have been like. But mostly we try to take care of ourselves as best we can in the belief that we are insignificant microbes in an indifferent universe. Being a child of this culture, I recognize and understand this point of view, but it is no longer my own. Years of reinterpreting experience and practicing disciplines of mind in harmony with a unified reality have caused me to see and experience life in other ways.

Traditional wisdom conceives of the Whole in terms of a single Creative Power acting on different levels through different means, or reflectors, to produce an infinite variety of creative results. In other words, everything that exists is the manifestation of a single source of Life and Being. My teachers were stubbornly and untiringly insistent on this point and I cannot be less so. Everything they had to say pointed back to this essential truth, just as every point on a circumference finds its meaning in the center.

One creative power acting on different fields produces different effects, and life is one of these effects. The creative energy is reflected in different ways depending on what embodies it. There is only one cosmic energy, but as this one energy meets various reflectors it is transformed into different capacities or qualities—just as different electrical appliances reflect a single electrical energy in the form of motion, sound, heat, and light. This creative energy stimulates all the processes of life in general and the whole range of human activity in particular. Everything reflects this one creative intelligence and power.

We do not experience this Creative Power directly, but know it only as it is reflected in our world and in us. Minerals, vegetative life, and animal life all reflect this same creative energy in different ways. Human life contains all the levels and qualities of the natural world, as well as manifestations of this energy that are distinctly human.

Because this energy is creative it produces effects that are beautiful, subtle, unexpected, and filled with life. Because it is one and of one source, it connects all things, from the galaxies to subatomic particles, within its greater purpose and meaning. Every grain of sand is numbered; nothing is isolated from the whole.

Energy is defined in physics as a capacity for doing work or overcoming resistance. We see the effects of energy in the flowering of plants as in the process of human reason, in the formation of minerals as in the evolution of culture, in the passing of a quarterback as in the flash of insight that brings a new understanding into focus. But the qualities of energy are different and can be arranged in a natural hierarchy that is self-evident once explained.

This energy reflected in the world of solids, or the mineral world, has the capacity and function of giving form, of holding things together. We can see its work in the formation of rocks and crystals. It has a kind of life and takes part in various molecular transformations. The world of solid forms, however, compared to higher levels of energy, possesses a very limited capacity for interaction.

On the level of vegetative or vital life this capacity for interaction increases. Vital life allows matter to take part in a much greater and more spontaneous interchange: sun, water, and minerals combine to form a rose in bloom. Vegetable and animal life come into existence and are maintained by vital energies.

As life gains greater complexity, an even greater freedom and capacity for response comes into play. A capacity in animal life allows new behavior to be learned and become a conditioned response. Certain behavior patterns arise through this learning capacity. If a certain behavior helps an animal to acquire the food it needs, that behavior will be learned, imprinted, becoming more of an automatic response. An animal that has an unpleasant experience through certain circumstances may try to avoid those circumstances. The human being, too, is programmed with a range of learned, conditioned responses that lie just beneath the threshold of awareness. This can be called the conditioning or automatic energy or capacity.

Beyond this lies the capacity of awareness, or sensitivity. This capacity, functioning in animals as well as humans, allows noticing and adaptation. With this quality of energy, life acquires an even greater possibility of responding to new situations. Whenever we do something with awareness, as if for the first time, rather than out of habit, we are using this capacity.

Awareness is characterized by attention being drawn to one of our functions—whether it be thought, emotion, physical sensation, or behavior. We notice something through having our attention drawn to it. Our attention is consumed by that which we notice: a fly on our nose, a beautiful person, a memory, a strong emotion. The attention is monopolized for a period of time, until something else attracts the attention.

This sensitivity brings attention to a single focus, but it does not yet allow for all our functions to be held within a wider field of awareness. Attention is monopolized by the content of awareness rather than widening to include the context that awareness can provide. On the level of sensitive energy we may still be fragmented, identified with a momentary experience, unaware of more than one part of ourselves at a time. For instance, a person may be so identified with a daydream that his or her immediate environment is for all purposes nonexistent. In the next moment something in the environment may grab the person's attention and the daydream may vanish from memory.

It is not until we come to true consciousness that we find a capacity that allows a wide field of awareness and thus a comprehensiveness to our perception and state of being. True consciousness opens us to wholeness, allowing a total experience of bodiliness, thought, and emotion. Everything is revealed in the more general light of conscious energy. Above all, there is a different sense of "I"—it is no longer the I that identifies with each passing impulse of sensation, thought, or emotion, but a transcending awareness, a witness that stands apart. With consciousness it is possible to direct one's attention and even to be conscious of where one's attention moves, to see moment by moment what attracts it.

Every higher level of energy allows more interaction and more freedom. If human beings are to reclaim their own latent capacities, this higher attention is needed.

With true consciousness, in contrast to passive awareness, the present moment is a wide space. Daydreams, nagging memories, the beckoning of an imaginary future have less of a hold on us, because the present is perceived as it is, in the perfection of its many dimensions. Consciousness is knowing that you *are*.

Presence is to have this quality of energy, this attention activated. In the present state of culture and conditioning, the state of presence is normally unavailable to people except as occasional flashes. It is possible, however, to cultivate consciousness, to sustain it, and to make our home in it.

As human beings we can know that a single creative energy connects everything and that we are integral to it. We are one with the Whole. This is the Truth on the highest level. We can also know that we have within us different capacities for reflecting this one energy. Our physical form is one type of reflection;

our ability to learn new kinds of behavior and physical skills is another. Our ability to notice and become aware of something is yet another capacity we are endowed with. But a critical distinction can be made between awareness and consciousness. A conscious presence is the perception from wholeness; it is the light of soul behind the fragmentation and unresolved conflicts of the personality. It can therefore unify and harmonize all other fragments and capacities, because it transcends them.

Consciousness is the highest capacity a human being can experience at will, and its importance is that it opens us up to what is beyond the individual will: the creative and enlivening powers of the Divine Unknown.

When a conscious presence has been awakened, giving us the ability to direct a refined attention, we are more able to open to the knowledge of the heart. The heart, as Sufis and others call it, is the totality of the mind's faculties, both sub- and supra-conscious.

These faculties work beyond the curtain of our conscious awareness. They function erratically, partially, and unconsciously in most of us, because the human heart is fragmented and in conflict.

If, however, the subconscious mind functions in harmony with the Divine Unknown, the Creative Power, life becomes filled with new meaning that flows into conscious awareness. Whereas awareness was occupied with more superficial layers of mind activity, particularly our ego's thoughts and desires, now it is possible to listen within more constantly. Through this listening, mind and heart, ego and subconscious can be integrated. Cosmic energy is being reflected by the subconscious faculties of the mind, which are able to reflect the new, the creative, the unexpected, and the unique.

To purify and harmonize our conscious and subconscious faculties, to make the heart pure around a single center, or master desire, and to patiently awaken those faculties that have gone to sleep or atrophied—this is the work of presence.

One day the heart may reach such contact with its own source through merging directly with the Creative Power and knowing the One behind multiplicity that it may make a home in unity. Human beings are destined to realize this possibility more and more. The result is the complete human being, the drop that becomes the Sea. It is not difficult to achieve this end, because we are made for it.

Balancing the Outer
and the Inner

Someone says, "I can't help feeding my family.
I have to work so hard to earn a living."
He can do without God, but not without food;
he can do without Religion,
but not without idols.
Where is one who'll say,
"If I eat bread without awareness of God,
I will choke."

RUMI, *MATHNAWI*, II, 3071–79

At one point in my journey, my teacher's teacher, an eighty-year-old man, had been in a serious car accident that had brought him near death. For months the master's condition was uncertain, causing all those who loved him to become acutely aware of what his living flesh-and-blood friendship meant to them. Eventually he would recover and live many more years. When he was well enough to barely walk, he phoned my teacher to tell him that he would have a special lesson if he could come to his apartment on a certain night. Since this was the first opportunity for the two of them to be together in months, my teacher was full of expectation.

They took a walk that evening, so slow and deliberate that it empha-
sized the attention required for each painful step. They walked as far as
one of the most elegant drinking establishments of that great city. My
teacher's teacher opened the door of that tavern and they entered. It was
as if they were perfectly invisible, while the patrons, the most fashionable
men and women, continued in their loud, intoxicated conversations.
"See?" he simply said.

In our ordinary state of being, both the outer demands of life
and the inner processes of thinking and feeling alternatively monopolize our attention to such an extent that we cannot sustain
true consciousness. By consciousness I mean not just perception
or awareness, which corresponds to the sensitive energy described earlier, but a field of awareness that includes both the
contents of an experience and the one who experiences.

Spiritual work involves maintaining some balance between
the demands of outer life and a conscious presence. We wish to
enter freely into the life of the world and still know presence, the
dimension of consciousness and freedom. We can live through
the essence, which is the light behind the personality, rather than
through the limited, superficial personality, which is identified
with each passing thought and feeling.

The personality is our superficial identity, our learned behavior and attitudes; it is tied to the conditions of outer life, to dis-
approval and approval, like and dislike, praise and blame. We are
working so that this essence, which can truly say "I am," may
come forward in the midst of life.

The personality, which is absorbed in the external world and
forgetful of the possibility of an inner life, is governed by that
world. All its inner events are tied to outer events and things. The
personality exists first of all in relation to other people and things
and wants to have its way with them. It feels its own existence
through what it achieves and what it possesses. Conversely, each
disappointment, each rejection, and each failure is experienced as
a challenge and threat to its own existence.

Are we consumed by the experiences of life? Or do we consciously experience life with mindfulness and trust? Is our inner life dependent on outer conditions, or is it becoming free of them?

The transformation with which inner work is concerned allows the "I" to exist more independently as a pure presence or witness. The slavery to like and dislike is diminished to the extent that our feeling of "I" is grounded in pure Being and not in things. The need to achieve our own specialness, for instance, or to receive attention from others, is experienced as less important as a stable inner presence develops. This inner presence is satisfying in itself; it enables nonattachment, equanimity, and greater objectivity.

Presence guides us to a healthy sense of self-restraint and self-sacrifice, enabling us to play with our attachments, to confront our own prison. We may learn to slip out of the stranglehold of egoism, which is based in desire and in the thoughts generated by desire. In being present to the play of desire we can diminish the ego's power over our inner being.

Eventually we reach a certain invulnerability in relation to outer things, so that we do not depend on them, but live from this presence instead. To look only outward is to miss the point, to stray from the straight path. It is to go begging for outer satisfactions, while we ignore the hidden treasure inside us.

We are knee deep in a river, searching for water. We are part of an invisible river, but we are so distracted by outer things and what we imagine they could mean to us that we lose contact with the source of our own Being. When we are caught in desire, in form, in externals, we are pulled out of ourselves into a fantasy world, a desire world. We lose touch with the invisible river, the waters of life, through our identification with unconscious inner processes and with outer demands.

There is an energy of attention that we at first have in only limited amounts. The loss of this energy has been described by the great thirteenth-century Sufi poet and saint Jelaluddin Rumi:

You have scattered your awareness in all directions,
and your vanities are not worth a bit of cabbage.
The root of every thorn
draws the water of your attention toward itself.
How will the water of your attention reach the fruit?
Cut through the evil roots, cut them away,
Direct the Bounty of God to spirit and to insight,
not to the knotted and broken world outside.
MATHNAWI, V, 1084–86

There is an energy of attention that must be conserved. Can we see ourselves throwing it away? Can we see ourselves wasting it on outer desire and satisfactions, intoxicated with the random demands of the ego, responding to all the needs of outer approval and validation? Our dependence on outer satisfactions and requirements leads us to envy, resentment, pride, guilt, and anger. Isn't this the contemporary idolatry?

Whoever makes all cares into a single care, the care for simply being present, will be relieved of all care by that Presence, which is the creative power. We can take a step back from the world of attraction, comparison, and dependence on externals, remember this vitality within us, and connect with it. Perhaps then we can be liberated from our compulsions and can learn to act through Spirit, rather than through our limited egos.

If remembering Presence becomes our single care, then we will waste less of our inner energy.

BALANCING SELF AND SELFLESSNESS

Another aspect of balance is between self and selflessness, between a strong presence and freedom from self. A common and shallow misunderstanding of the spiritual process consists in wanting to move directly from being an ego-driven individual to

having "no self." But discovering our own presence is the beginning of being free of the compulsive and demanding ego.

The essence of the spiritual process is sustaining presence.
Presence is our very Self. It is a space to be filled by the qualities of
Spirit—qualities such as love, generosity, patience, courage, humility, and wisdom, which are inclusive, encompassing, and transcendent. The ego is a crowded space filled with conflicting desires and thoughts.

Sometimes we want to begin spiritual work but are too filled.
Every word, movement, and thought invokes some artificial "I,"
some conditioning or superficial role. When we come into Presence, we enter speechlessness, silence. We put our weapons
down. The intellect is given rest; thoughts subside. Then the feelings, too, can become still and empty.

Our work is to cross a threshold into emptiness and stillness.
It is like entering an empty room that proves to hold a great presence. The apparent emptiness of simple presence is richer than
the crowded experience of ordinary personality. We can either
be empty with Spirit or full of ourselves.

The barriers before us include our thoughts and emotions,
our psychic and worldly busyness, and our house of idols, occupying us to no end. Our habits and conditioning keep us intoxicated and dull. If we accept the barriers, we fail to cross the
threshold. To cross the threshold from habits and conditioning to
emptiness, which is the receptive quality of the soul, we must become still and patient. We must give up certain impulses and let
go again and again. This is the way in which we come into our
Self. We leave behind our compulsive egos, embodying the "I
Am" and selflessness at the same time.

The "I Am" is not the mechanical self—the role-playing, superficial personality—that feels its existence through its ordinary
reactions and resistances. With the right kind of attention and
observation we can see the relationship between our various
thoughts and sentiments and how each of them invokes some

imaginary "I." We can learn to feel our own existence through presence and intention. A positive sense of "I-ness" emerges through recollection. It is the first thing we can *trust*: our own presence, the sacred "I Am."

The apparent conflict between a strong sense of our own presence and selflessness can be resolved if we realize that presence helps us to be more selfless. Selflessness is the soul's own willingness to make sacrifices in the material world, as well as in the artificial world of personality. The "I Am" is selfless in that it holds no special idea of itself, does not justify itself, and is not envious, resentful, or proud. Because it already feels secure in the infinitely merciful Spirit, it can accept the annihilation of what is false in the ego personality. If we are in submission to Self, we are capable of letting go of the demands of the ego. If we are not secure in the emptiness of Self, we will cling to events and things, to lies and fears. Free of the coercions of the ego, we can become our authentic selves.

The Power of Being

God has made nonexistence appear solid and re-
spectable;
and He has made Existence appear in the guise of
nonexistence.
He has hidden the Sea and made the foam visible,
He has concealed the Wind and shown you the
dust.

RUMI, MATHNAWI, V, 1026–27

 There is something nonexistent, something that cannot
be touched, seen, or even thought, and yet this nothing
is more important than anything else, the fathomless
source of all qualities and all possibilities.

We look for happiness, beauty, or pleasure in existing things,
convinced that things will satisfy us or bring us desirable states.
We hope to find well-being in a new car, a new place to live, or a
new relationship. But the happiness produced by these things
cannot be counted on to last, and we will need to find yet other
things to stimulate further states.

What we have within ourselves we project outward onto
things, thinking that the things themselves are responsible for the
states we experience. Yet every state is nevertheless *within* us. If
we truly come to know ourselves and what we carry within, if

we can make contact with ourselves directly, we will be less dependent on things. The well-being, the beauty, and the love we seek outside of ourselves is truly within. The paradox is that as we discover what is within, the outer things will increasingly awaken these inner qualities. We will respond more readily; we will appreciate more, love more, and know a greater sense of independent well-being.

Everything that seems to exist, both in the material and psychological worlds, derives its qualities from a single source of Being. Everything we desire, everything that motivates us is in reality without any existence of its own and depends on a single source of Being. All things receive their qualities and their existence from this single source of Life and are only reflectors of that one Essence.

Furthermore, what attracts us in the outer world is only putting us in touch with the hidden treasure within ourselves. Through finding it in ourselves we are returned to the Being that we reflect. We are not the originators of qualities, but the reflectors of the infinite qualities of Being.

A fundamental unity underlies all of existence. Existence is a gift from Divine Mercy, from Being itself, which allows all things to exist in their exquisite interplay. Yet all these existing things absorb and monopolize our attention and concern. They delude and seduce us. Because they appear to be many, they tear the heart to pieces and fragment the will. If we do not find a way to carry the unity with us, we will know only chaos and confusion.

Paradoxically, what is needed is an ability to reserve some attention for Being itself, for what is not existent in the world of things. We can give attention to that dimension that allows all things to exist. In the midst of all the things that are calling for our attention, we must simultaneously remember a center that is nowhere and everywhere, that is the source and substance of everything that seems to exist and be, and that has a point of contact accessible to us. Within the heart of each human being is a point of contact with the immeasurable dimension outside of all existing things. God, the Absolute, is not another existing thing among other existing things, but the dimension that makes all existences possible and from which they derive their Being. It is for this reason that God is said to be nearer to us than our jugular vein.

The straight and narrow path is a path of fastidious remembrance of Being. Any way is insufficient that does not recognize and emphasize the need for the awareness of Being in each moment—for a presence that is independent of bias, limiting concepts, comparisons, reactivity, and sentimentality. For in any moment we may find that our presence is absorbed in some secondary event or thing. If we forget this source of Being, we may eventually forget ourselves. What is lost, one might ask, if we allow ourselves to be absorbed in things, in feelings, in thoughts—in all this excitement?

Without Being our activity becomes chaotic, delinquent, purposeless, and wasteful. Any act without the fragrance of Being is lost. Being is the integrity of every thing. Being is like a finer energy that has the power to organize coarser energies; it is more energized than any activity or function and is larger than life. It is a creative energy behind our actions. No effort, activity, attraction, or satisfaction in itself is Being. Being calls from another direction, from the world of possibility beyond our awareness.

Being is the domain of quality. Whatever we do with Being embodies qualities and attributes more purely and intensely. We can bring quality into the details of life if we remember to be and act with precision. If we can *be* at that point where the horizontal force of active choice meets the vertical force of Being, a certain "something," larger than life, will be activated. This "something" can be felt in anything produced by the hands and heart of a human being—in works of art, in a well-tended garden, and in food prepared with love.

"Though you possess two hundred existences, become non-existent in His Being—it is right to become nonexistent for that Being," writes Rumi in his *Divan*. The awakening to Being requires emptying oneself. But this emptying allows for a new quality of relationship and an alchemical transformation of energies.

A master of Balinese dance once expressed the idea that a performer must consciously see himself as a channel between the world within and the world outside. If the ego gets in the way, this channeling is reduced. He described a ball of energy that is created between performers and their audiences. The performers consciously manipulate and expand this energy force using the attention that is given to them by the audience and which they control. By being a pure channel and through their skill of relating to the audience, the energy is moved back and forth. In sacred art, performance is not a means of ego gratification but an offering to the Divine. What is offered is everyone's attention, and yet everyone is elevated in this sacred alchemy and feels a change of consciousness through this quality of performance and the attention offered. The offering to the Divine is returned.

· Every relationship can have this quality if we offer ourselves willingly, if we accept that we are channels, and if we accept being empty and aware. This is charisma, or the ability of putting into action the Divine attributes of the subconscious mind.

The One in its unlimited Generosity and Compassion initiates remembering in us and begins the process of completion. Its offering its Being to us is its Mercy. This *Isness*, this Mercy—whatever name we give to It—came before us. We arose out of it, not it out of us. Or as it is said: God's love for us preceded our love for Him. As much as we are the servants of Spirit, Spirit is our servant when we make our connection to It. This connection is made through presence, which is a receptivity to the energies of possibility.

When our teacher from Turkey came to Washington National Airport, something quite unusual happened. Suleyman Dede was a small man who dressed impeccably in a three-piece suit and could have been someone's grandfather from any Middle Eastern or Mediterranean country. There was little in his outward appearance to make him stand out, and yet the whole airport was practically silenced by his presence passing through it. In a lounge area where he and his wife had to wait for awhile with their two American guides and translators, strangers came up to him and started telling him about their lives or asked him important questions.

Once, as Dede brought us to "meet" Mevlana at the Konya Tekkye, now a museum, people—mostly Turkish peasants—began to gather around him until a rather large crowd was moving from Mevlana's tomb, to the turning hall, to the rose garden. Such is the power and attraction of Being.

Voluntary Attention

If your thought is a rose,
you are a rose garden;
if it is a thorn,
you are fuel for the bath stove.

RUMI, *MATHNAWI*, II, 278

Why study attention? What is the faculty of attention? It could almost be said that a human being *is* attention. Whatever occupies our attention—whether inwardly or outwardly, whether profound or trivial—is what we are at that moment. Therefore, if we are attentive only to the outer world, we forfeit our own inner life. On the other hand, if we are excessively introverted, we cut ourselves off from the impressions of the outer world that could enrich and enliven us. If we attend only to the material world, we sacrifice the spiritual. If we think we can focus exclusively on the spiritual, we might lose ourselves in a world of dreams that never connect with reality. We need not only attention but balance—balance between the narrow and the wide, the outer and the inner, the material and the spiritual.

Life requires so much of us that none of us can afford to be without our full attention. More often than we know, moments come that will make a difference to the quality of our lives. These are moments of choice that will never come again. They are moments of service, because others need our presence and attention, and moments of understanding in a world of much misunderstanding.

The study of attention is also the study of the ego and the essential Self. One of the qualities of the ego is that it has little attention of its own; instead, its attention is captured and compelled by what it likes and dislikes. The awakened Self, on the other hand, can direct and sustain attention.

Observe how much of our attention is absorbed in the struggle between like and dislike. Attention roams freely and unconsciously until it strikes on something that either attracts or repulses it; then it is caught. Presence allows us to notice how and when attention is caught and how to free it again. As we begin to see what compels our attention and why, we also weaken the tyranny of the ego and begin to create an impartial observer.

In our inner world we can learn to notice identification—the involuntary and unconscious absorption of our attention in inner processes. We tell ourselves we will be patient, kind, or generous; then, in another moment, we have forgotten this because some desire or frustration has so captured us that we have lost our observing attention and are racing out of control in just that state we intended to avoid. We have lost ourselves through identification.

On the other hand, there may be times when we choose to identify ourselves with something. We may want to identify with a feeling of joy or love, to play with a child, or to act as if we are a horse. This conscious, intentional identification can have a positive value in our lives, but this value consists precisely in its being conscious and voluntary.

At the end of a day of conscious work my teacher would say, "Maybe now you have a little free attention." Free attention is a power of the soul that throws light on whatever it meets. It develops when the soul begins to give itself out through its attention. At first it may require great and systematic efforts to be developed.

We know how difficult it can be to pay attention. At the moment that we notice something, there is no effort. Effort enters when we try to sustain attention. We can bring ourselves to a state of attention, but we cannot keep it from dissolving. Our capacity for voluntary attention is small.

The source of attention is outside of time, but under the temporal conditions in which the human mind usually functions, attention is disturbed and dispersed. If we are truly gathered at the center of our own Being, higher energies of our psyche are able to organize the lower energies and lend them a coherence they in themselves lack. But, at the same time, the lower energies (all the impacts of environment and conditioning) are able to disorganize the higher ones and introduce into them something of the incoherence of the lower levels. Out of this dynamic comes the struggle to keep our attention on something.

The world is governed by people capturing one another's attention. Unless we develop some capacity for free attention, we are the prey of those who can monopolize attention in the political and economic domains.

We need to look at the possibility of a voluntary attention in which we ourselves are taking the initiative. Voluntary attention is not completely determined by our reactions to outside stimuli. If we cannot tell the difference between voluntary and involuntary attention, we are living in a dream world. Work with attention enters into all work on oneself. To "act from oneself" is the measure of real will.

It is our responsibility to use our everyday conditions as an opportunity for the development of attention. We can learn to develop attention in at least four major directions: the outer and the inner, the narrow and the wide.

We can begin with attention to the sensations of our own

physical organism, because sensation is the interface between the outer and the inner, the material and the psychological. We can sustain a sense of our physical presence through being aware of sense impressions: sound, touch, smell, and the sense of our own bodiliness, especially our breathing.

We can notice how our attention moves between the outer world and our inner world. The outer world is the source of all kinds of impressions that we can receive more consciously. The more we consciously receive these impressions, the more we will be enlivened by them, because they are a kind of food for the nervous system and can be better digested with the "enzymes" of conscious awareness.

The inner world includes thoughts, emotions, and subtler psychic impressions. With presence we can overcome our unconscious identification with these processes and know ourselves as we are. We can avoid becoming the victims of our own unconscious processes. Just as we can consciously release physical tensions through our awareness of the body and its postures, we can also release emotional tensions by recognizing them. As with physical tensions, our emotional tensions have greater power over us the more they are unconscious. Bringing our attention fully and willingly to emotional contractions and blockages has a transformative power. The validity of the current psychological technique known as focusing is based in the self-healing power of voluntary attention. In fact much of the effectiveness of any psychotherapy, independent of the models and beliefs of the therapist, is the quality of therapeutic attention that is realized together by the therapist and client. It may be the most important contribution of the therapist to teach another how to attend to inner emotional states and processes.

Presence allows a two-way attention that is the essence of relationship and communication. With this two-way attention we can be simultaneously aware of our inner state and the state of another.

Sometimes we are so totally identified with our own feelings that we are not capable of being in a relationship. At other times we may lose ourselves in the state of another, especially when it is negative, and not be able to separate ourselves from the problem enough to be objective. In relationships this monitoring of outer and inner attention can help us to be more sensitive to others and more aware of our own feelings at the same time.

We can also attend with a wide or a narrow focus. As is appropriate to the needs of the moment, we can either open up or concentrate. What a joy it is to widen the aperture of consciousness so that while walking through nature we have a global sense of *being* there, and what a joy to focus on a detail that we have *chosen!* What a pleasure it is to open up to a panoramic sense of presence! This is the joy of being fully human, of taking responsibility for the capacity of our own attention.

Gradually we learn to sustain a focus with steadiness and continuity, with patience and interest. We should be able to construct an intentional image or maintain a state of receptivity. This observing stabilizes itself as an inner presence. This stable inner presence then becomes a source and ground of attention itself.

What we choose to give our attention to we energize. We should accept certain impressions and not dwell on others. The more conscious we can make this process, the less we will energize those things that conflict with our well-being and values. Attention develops as the gatekeeper of all our impressions.

We learn not to let the mind wander too far from the essential Self, even while we are open to outer things. More and more we work to keep our attention on Being itself. We can learn to call upon a very refined attention, to keep an awareness of the deepest truths in the most ordinary circumstances. This can be done only if our attention is not easily coerced and distracted. As we begin to develop an independent attention, one that can look outward and inward at the same time, we begin to acquire the presence that is the enabling factor of all spiritual work.

38

The training of the attention is a necessary part of our spiritual training. It is an essential factor in the mind spiritualizing itself, in the development of the soul. Eventually, attention may become luminous and creative. It directs the power of the soul. As we consciously give our attention to others—to creative acts and to service—we are also giving of our soul, and this is how the soul grows.

I remember days of difficult labor in a spiritual school where we were encouraged to keep a balanced attention through all kinds of situations. I was given the task of grooming a horse. From mane to tail, from the hooves right up, I worked for hours. Then the teacher came and after a brief inspection said, "Very poor job, superficial and sloppy." He and I watched as my heart sank. But then something rebounded: I knew I had done my best; I knew that I could not be a slave of reward or blame. In that moment, I saw the twinkle in his eye as he turned and left.

Meditation:
The Refinement of
Attention

In this world you have become clothed and rich,
but when you come out of this world, how will you be?
Learn a trade that will earn you forgiveness.
In the world beyond there's also traffic and trade.
Beside those earnings, this world is just play.
As children embrace in fantasy intercourse,
or set up a candy shop, this world is a game.
Night falls, and the child
comes home hungry without his friends.

RUMI, *MATHNAWI*, II, 2593–99

The religious conditioning of my youth had created in me an image of a universe divided between Heaven and Hell, between redemption and damnation. Heaven was the destination of the virtuous, who were mostly those who had been saved by belief in the doctrines of the Church. Once I had certain experiences that showed me deeper levels of reality and the mind, this conditioning lost its power over me. I simply could not take it seriously, because it did not correspond with the levels of reality I had experienced. I experienced a cosmic love and meaningfulness, but the clouds of Heaven or gates of Hell were nowhere in sight. There was a self-created Hell, the illusions constructed by our habitual desires and patterns of false thinking; and there was a fundamental, underlying reality that felt whole and beneficent. I began to search for an explanation that made sense.

The rather naïve image that developed in my mind was one of the enlightened being, free of illusion and desire. The means of becoming such a being was meditation, the practice of emptying the mind of every desire and thought until Reality shone through in all its brilliance and one was enlightened. This would best be done away from the world, preferably under circumstances that were arranged to support this emptying process—an ashram, a *zendo,* or a cave. I thought that the highest spiritual attainment, the ultimate fulfillment of our human possibilities was this liberation from the suffering that thoroughly occupied the whole of humanity.

Meanwhile I was occupied with meeting my own material and emotional needs through jobs, relationships, and entertainments. When I first encountered the teachings of the Fourth Way, through a group that lived the teachings rather than just reading about them, I realized that I had found a bridge between that high ideal of liberation and the facts of my everyday life in the world.

The Fourth Way is a term introduced by G. I. Gurdjieff to describe the spiritual path of someone who lives and works within society, in contrast to the way of the ascetic, the monk, and the yogi, who traditionally separate themselves from ordinary life. Increasingly in the West ordinary lay people are undertaking the spiritual practices that were formerly the province of specialists. The Fourth Way, however, has been the primary way within the Islamic world for fourteen centuries.

The image that developed was what is termed the conscious man, who though in the world was not of it, who lived his life practically but without identification, and who "remembered" himself always and everywhere. Through work on himself, this conscious man could wake up in the midst of life and so free himself from the "terror of the situation" that was the unconscious mechanicality in which most human beings lived out their lives. If this sounds elitist, it probably is, but it gave me a starting point I could take seriously. I didn't need to give up all desires and thoughts; I needed to free myself from my identification with them, and then I would be in contact with the higher capacities that these identifications obscured.

After some years of giving myself to these teachings I felt that I had developed my attention and my presence, but I was noticing that self-remembering did not necessarily guarantee that my relationships would be healthy or that the qualities I respected as a human being—loving kindness, generosity, forgiveness, integrity—would develop. On the contrary, I witnessed the development in me of a tendency toward amorality and aloofness.

Sufism was the antidote that I found to cure myself of the preoccupation with myself that had developed in the name of becoming a conscious man. Sufism said, "All is Love and all is God: lose your self in this Love, but tether your camel, serve your guest, cook your meals, work and profit from your work." Sufism seemed to be an integration of freedom from thoughts and desires, on the one hand, with service and practicality, on the other. In some ways it returned to me an appreciation of the realness of virtues and sin. Sin was separation from the One, a state that veiled us from the Real. As virtue created Heaven, sin created Hell, although these states were present in the here and now as well as "hereafter."

Throughout this journey, meditation—the focusing of attention on subtler levels of Being—has been a constant. It is neither the ultimate pastime nor the only tool for spiritual development, but it deserves clear recognition as a principle of spiritual living.

What characterizes the human being is a gift of conscious awareness that offers us the possibility of real will and creativity, as well as the opportunity to know the source of this conscious awareness, the Spirit from which it emanates. Usually, however, this conscious awareness is absorbed in experience and embedded in the structures of perception. This is life as most people know it: the complete identification of one's awareness with all the events and subjective experiences that life on earth offers. This consciousness is also identified with a self-construct, an ego that is ruled by contradictory desires and conditionings.

Although many people in our society have experienced this freedom from identification, many fewer value this conscious awareness enough to make the efforts necessary to achieve it. To value going beyond this identification of consciousness with experience represents a major breakthrough, although a significant number of people have had this breakthrough in recent decades. It causes one to evaluate one's life in a new way—to observe one's thoughts, feelings, and actions and see their results with a new objectivity. One realizes the degree of unconscious suffering that ordinary life represents and begins to acquire a new attitude of remembrance or mindfulness. The expectations one has about life change: fulfillment comes less from material or ego satisfactions and more from the transformation of perception through awareness. The quality of life begins to change, and lifestyle and behavior change to support and accommodate this new focus on awareness. Certain forms of unconscious behavior cost us too much in terms of our ability to make efforts of awareness, and so they are left behind.

Although the best way to approach meditation is with a qualified teacher, a mature meditator with whom one can resonate, some basic knowledge can be profitably offered in a book like this. Even advanced meditators often benefit by being reminded of the very simplicity of meditation itself.

The simplest form of meditation requires two things: a body that is still and relaxed, and an object to focus attention on. Many traditional postures for meditation exist. I have found the greatest ease and stability sitting in a chair, with the spine erect and the palms of the hands resting on the knees. The focus of attention that I have found most useful for beginners is the awareness of breathing combined with a mental focus: "I" as a feeling in the heart with each inhalation and "am" as a sensation of the whole physical presence on the exhalation. As attention is held on this process, the breathing becomes calmer and the internal dialog begins to settle down. From this position of quiet alertness it becomes possible to view the stream of consciousness. The awareness that in normal living is focused outward gets accustomed to an inward focus. This focus, however, is less on the content than on the process of the mind's activity. Awareness has begun to separate from its identification with the content of both outward and inward experience.

In much of our ordinary life we are busy interpreting experience and constructing meanings. Our perceptions are also biased by expectation, opinion, desire, and many other factors. During meditation we use more energy to sustain the process of seeing and very little for interpretation and constructing meanings. The net effect of this kind of meditation practice is that we reduce our reactivity and increase our ability to sustain pure awareness.

At a higher stage of meditation the focus of awareness becomes more subtle. Instead of focusing on a breath, a sound, or an idea, consciousness attends to *Being* itself. Instead of change, consciousness focuses on that which is changeless, the underlying "Isness." This substratum of consciousness becomes more and more familiar. Instead of the contents of the mirror, we are aware of the mirror itself.

Everyday life is seen more and more as a reflection of the mirror—as both real and unreal against the backdrop of this underlying changeless reality. Meditation at this level is experienced as much by a letting go as by a firm concentration. As the object of consciousness becomes more subtle, so does the effort of consciousness.

Consciousness attends to whatever arises. Meditation is more and more carried into the gross psychological events of ordinary life. At this stage some of our compulsions have been recognized and can fall away. The compulsive habits of thought—many of them based on fear, desire, neediness, and self-centeredness—begin to lose their power. The identity that was rooted in these compulsions begins to melt and a new quality of "I" emerges, one based in simple nonreactive awareness. A different, less egotistical self begins to be felt.

Freed of our habitual thoughts, expectations, opinions, constructions, and fears, consciousness is freed to receive deeper impressions. New meanings begin to flow into consciousness from the unconscious. Extrasensory experience may be heightened. Whether we are aware of it or not, we become more sensitive to others' thoughts and emotions. We may be able to respond to others more sensitively and wisely, because we are less dominated by our old habitual patterns of thought and feeling. At this stage we are flooded with rich meanings, and life can take on a new depth.

There really is no end to the refinement that is possible. One more and more begins to perceive qualitatively. The ultimate reality, which we are preparing to apprehend and which is all that is, has certain qualities such as peace, compassion, creativity, vitality, generosity, glory, subtlety, wisdom, beauty, and unity.

Through this deeper refinement of attention and an ever more subtle focusing, the false identity collapses. The supports on which it once depended have been removed, and the self begins to feel like a unique point of view of the Whole, a reflector of cosmic awareness.

The Tyranny
of the False Self

Save us from what our own hands might do;
lift the veil, but do not tear it.
Save us from the ego; its knife has reached our
  bones.
Who but You will break these chains?
Let us turn from ourselves to You
Who are nearer to us than ourselves.
Even this prayer is Your gift to us.
How else has a rose garden grown from these
  ashes?

RUMI, *MATHNAWI*, II, 2443–49

Almost before it is possible to understand the significance of a spiritual life, we must look at the psychological conditionings that characterize our inner life. A spiritual teaching is to some extent a critique of personality and conventional social conditioning. It challenges the conventional view of the human personality. It calls to us from another level—the truly human level—asking us to transcend our fear, limitation, judgment, envy, resentment, and false pride. It offers to lead us beyond the stimulus-response syndrome, beyond aggressive-defensive behavior, beyond the sleep of conditioning, and beyond the slavery to the ego. It offers a very high vision of what a human being is.

The lower self does not know that it is asleep; consequently, what appreciation can it have for awakening? It consists of our fears and defenses, likes and dislikes, expectations, opinions, attitudes, and preoccupations, and we take it to be ourselves. This self could be called the compulsive or defensive self. It wants whatever will support its illusions, and it hates and fears whatever threatens its illusions.

We who have been born into these times face conditions that make the search for truth difficult: belief systems that carry guilt and fear, cultural and religious taboos, clichés of pseudospirituality and popular psychology, and a muddle of irrelevant concepts. Many of our assumptions and ways of thinking might have to go through the fire of rigorous examination. We have belief systems that carry unnecessary guilt, fear, and cultural or religious taboos that may be out of harmony with human nature. The idea that there is a God who exists to mete out punishment to sinners has created more alienation than moral awareness. The notion that sex is dirty has subconsciously disturbed relationships that could otherwise be healthy and joyful.

Furthermore, we need to be aware of the clichés of pseudospirituality that pose as wisdom and elements of popular psychology that merely stroke the false self. Some of these are a reaction against the excessive burden of guilt that has been inflicted on us by many religions. Some are the superficial concepts that good and evil exist only in our minds, or that anything someone may do is right for them—that there is little or no objective morality—or that all we can know is that we don't know.

We face a muddle of irrelevant concepts patched together from knowledge borrowed from those who pretended to know.

At this time, however, there are particular needs that need to be taken into account that make transcendence of the ego even more complicated and sensitive.

Women who have been taught to deny their own needs in favor of their families or in deference to men will be sensitive to the suggestion that they should look beyond their personal needs and desires, or that service is the natural expression of the soul. What may be the remedy for pervasive human egoism may only increase the disease unless a person understands that the compulsive, guilt ridden denial of one's individuality is quite different from a healthy transcendence of the self. The former is unconscious; the latter is possible only when one has come to understand one's essential needs and that satisfying these needs is not necessarily the same as ego-gratification.

Our culture has experienced a plague of childhood victimization, which has only recently begun to come into the light of collective awareness. A significant percentage of us have been raised in dysfunctional families that ignored the fundamental need of the child to experience an environment of love, support, and trust. Perhaps the two greatest factors that have contributed to childhood victimization and abuse have been alcoholism (and other addictions) and the sexual pathology of our culture.

To say that the self has no boundaries could be misunderstood by someone who has had their boundaries violated in dysfunctional or incestuous families. The point is not that one has no boundaries and is therefore defenseless and available to anything. On the contrary, it is that one's individuality can be so centered in Spirit that it becomes a subtle, expansive, and healing presence.

Alcoholism and other addictions have deprived many children of having their needs met and have forced these same children to be the numbed care-givers of their own parents. In this process many people have forgotten their own needs and have thus missed an important step in their ego development. They have forgotten themselves before they have found themselves. It is premature to speak of self-transcendence before someone has a viable ego.

Our prevailing sexual attitudes are simultaneously promiscuous and puritanical. We broadcast sexual imagery from every direction, sanction it, and intensify its power over us, but never recognize its appropriate place in human relationships. However, we also see sexuality as dirty and sinful. Once the connection between sex and evil is made, sexuality will be associated with other evils—selfish manipulation, wanton excess, and even physical abuse. Because we have forgotten the golden rule of sexuality—that it is the merging of equals—we see it as merely a means of gratifying desire regardless of the consequences to the other person. This is the process that gradually leads to the possibility of parents using their children as sex objects. People who have had their personal boundaries violated in this way will need their individuality to be healed. Fortunately, the essential Self of a human being cannot be permanently damaged; as much as it may be caused to shrink back or hide, it remains essentially unharmed and unspoiled.

If a person has a history of this kind of victimization, however, there is the possibility of misunderstanding the transformation of the ego. One danger is that the person will strive very hard in spiritual disciplines as a way of avoiding or burying deep pain. Eventually, however, it will be realized that the spiritual path must bring everything to light.

Another possible complication is that such people will be so wounded in their self-esteem that they will get stuck in a perpetual search for mere comfort and reassurance of the limited personality. Here, of course, there is a danger of being diverted or of never taking the steps that will lead to freedom.

A balanced spiritual teaching will include ideas and practices for both integrating and transcending the self. A healthy functional ego is needed to be able to face the deprivations and wounds of the personality. An integrated presence allows one to open up the painful feelings and disturbing memories and to allow them to be healed by the energies of the essential Self. Eventually, however, the false self—the ego—needs to be exposed and understood.

Our post-industrial, materialistic, secularized culture does not encourage the awakening of our essential Self. Widespread consumerism, self-indulgence, habits of immediate gratification, the moral relativity of our age, and the displacement of individual and communal responsibilities by large corporations, institutions, and bureaucracies bring us fewer moments of truth, fewer encounters with our essential and authentic Selves. The distraction of entertainments that appeal to every human weakness and the pervasive artificiality that technologies have brought leave us little chance of being what we are meant to be.

It may be difficult to appreciate the Work at first, but once its significance has been grasped, it becomes central to our lives. What will carry us through is the understanding that this Work leads to real well-being rather than illusory self-gratification.

THE FALSE SELF

Somewhere, somehow, we began to live as if we were separate, alone, and in danger. Once afraid, we constructed a self out of that fear and have been steadfastly defending it ever since. This false self exists in the intellect—in other words, in our thoughts, and particularly those thoughts that have been generated by fear and the desires that fear creates. It has developed and come between ourselves and objective reality. This totality of acquired fears, habits, preferences, and opinions must be exposed and understood.

When the false self divorces itself from the heart, or subconscious mind, and begins to acquire autonomy, it loses contact with its own source of Being and integrity. The false self can be understood as intellect struggling for its own survival at the expense of the whole mind.

A fixation on the false, compulsive self can distort our sense of reality, of justice, of balance. Again and again this false self can ruin things for the *whole* of oneself. The real possibility of the moment is destroyed from too much self-importance as well as from too little self-respect, from greed as well as from indifference, and from our disorderly desires as well as from inertia. Following the impulses of this false self, our essential Self is more and more eclipsed.

We are slaves to a tyrant called "ego." Unless we are extremely astute we do not see the extent to which we are controlled by our habits, compulsions, and desires, because we are working so hard to satisfy their random expectations.

The ego can be useful as a servant and a messenger, handling our affairs in the world according to the instructions and guidance it receives through the heart, from the higher Self. But without spiritual presence and intention we may not be able to distinguish the guidance of the heart from the impulses of our egoism. Without awakening the will, we cannot understand what is needed in any moment.

For this reason, various situations that require patience, humility, and service and that reorient our awareness are offered to those who have committed themselves to the Work of awakening. It may take special methods of effort and intention in order for this fixation on the false self to be brought into relief, but once seen and realized, our wish to awaken intensifies, and we never sleep as easily again.

OBJECTIVE SEEING

The work to become free of the false self that obscures the essential Self is accomplished through loving but objective observation. It is necessary to see oneself with other than one's habitual eyes—that is, differently from our usual way of looking at things. Unless we can see ourselves with some impartiality, our fixation on the false ego will only continue to block any objective understanding. All that is now called mind and feeling must be observed through new eyes. This new quality of seeing is by means of the eyes of the heart, and the light by which they see is both concentrated and transmitted by an authentic teaching and the resonance of a group.

We have a power of reason that can discern our egoism from our true Self, and because of this, we have the possibility of transcending our egoism in the name of love and attaining the true meaning of our individuality. A certain energy needs to be produced; a light needs to be kindled. Spirit will put a light before us, but not until we have taken a step, if only one step, from our egoism.

By keeping the mirror of awareness clear we can begin to free ourselves of our compulsions and inappropriate thoughts and behavior. Awareness is the means; the present moment is the focus. We have certain obstacles to face. We must confront our lack of attention and weakness of will, our attachment to our opinions, our slavery to our likes and dislikes, and our perpetual fear of loss. All of these characteristics form the gross material for the work of transformation, to be transformed by the resonance of love, the power of our essential Self. It is necessary to awaken to this Self, which has the power of love that can tame the false self.

TRANSFORMATION THROUGH LOVE

A teacher of mine once said, "Egotism is the bastard child of an affair between intellect and selfish desire." Our thinking mind, or intellect, can marry three forms of love: desire (Eros), friendship (*philos*), or unconditional love (*agape*). Actually, all three forms of love coexist.

THE TYRANNY OF THE FALSE SELF

The first form, desire, is what predominates in the false self. The false self is the "I" motivated by selfish desire, rather than by the wholeness of love. Desire, which is the ego's love of the desirable, can coexist with cosmic love and be balanced by it. It is negative only when it displaces the other forms of love, when it enslaves us and overcomes our better judgment.

Governed by the desires of ego we can feel very self-confident, righteous, and justified in our actions. We can have very strong opinions and can feel that we are right and the rest of the world is wrong. Excessive ambition, greed, lust, envy, self-righteousness, self-importance, and arrogance are all the results of excessive ego, the "I" as it is governed by desire.

Most negative states are the result of frustration—the frustration of desire, expectation, and love. Because egotism is the child of intellect married to desire, it is the frustration of desire that produces the negative states of the ego: anger, resentment, cynicism, hatred, bitterness, loneliness, and anxiety. Hatred, after all, is only frustrated love. In observing any strongly negative state we can see that the ego has been frustrated.

What is so useful about this scheme of the three forms of love is that it gives us an idea of how we can transform the ego from being a desire-driven, obsessive, and frustrated force to a transformed identity that is in touch with reality. Practically speaking, if we can shift our orientation from the exclusive concentration on satisfying our desires, to a love of sharing in friendship, and a cosmic love that sees others as ourselves, then our identity, or ego, is transformed by these loves.

THE COMMUNITY OF THE EGOLESS

Friendship, service, and communion can lead to cosmic love. Ambition, envy, or even self-improvement can lead in an altogether different direction when it is not balanced by a sense of we-ness. There is a danger in being too alone, in trying to satisfy ourselves exclusively.

In order to recognize the ego you have to be familiar with the non-ego. Individuals who are made gentle by love, who puts others' needs before their own, who neither judge others nor themselves too harshly, who do not consider themselves above others, who are not affected by the opinions of others, and who do not even desire to be virtuous are relatively free of egotism. The rest of us are slaves to it.

Egotism is difficult to see when we most need to see it; this is because we are identified with it at the moment that it has its greatest effect on us. The ego has many modalities:

> Some of us are performers; all we need is to have the attention of others and we begin to puff up with self-importance. The desire is to prove that we are better than others.
>
> Some of us are martyrs who enjoy the wrongs we imagine others are doing to us because they feed the strangely pleasurable sensation of self-pity.
>
> Some of us are always busy; we constantly pursue our mundane and heartless goals, which we consider more important than sharing time with others. We hide behind our busyness and, fixated on a limited, isolated self, we avoid relationships.
>
> Some of us are cynics, never free of a critical attitude toward others. Perhaps frustrations have left us powerless, and our only defense is this cynicism.
>
> Some of us are murderers, murdering others in our minds, thriving on anger and judgment, never willing to credit good to anyone.
>
> Some of us are angry because others have not fulfilled our expectations. This usually means they have not shown us the degree of importance we feel we deserve.

All of these modalities arise from a denial of love. The only way to deal with such separation is to step back and recall what drew us into relationships in the first place, assume some good-will, and be humble enough to consider our own faults. This can free us of the "I-thought." Eventually we can learn to be more and more free of our self-centered thoughts and expectations, asking little of others except what they are, seeing the best in them, and showing patience and tolerance.

Egotism is the very devil itself, a limitless source of envy, re-sentment, and pride. A healthy passion for life is a gift, but we need not let this passion become fixated on the desires of the lim-ited self.

We can transform this egotism by substituting more of "we-ness" in place of "I-ness." We can cultivate the "we-feeling" and feel our strength and value in our relationships.

Some of us use spirituality to increase self-importance and specialness. We cover egotism with the appearance of humility and selfishness with the appearance of generosity.

We have to get right down to the fundamental changes in ourselves that are necessary, and this requires sincerity. We be-come free of the self-motive by becoming nothing. And we can become nothing by limiting our habitual self-centered thoughts. This will cut at the roots of our egotism, as ego exists in our thinking. Habitual, unconscious thought may be motivated by desire, fear, or frustration. If we can regularly experience at least a relative freedom from egotistic thought by intentionally inter-rupting the habit of mechanical thinking, by entering into direct perception and presence, we can undermine the structure of fear and selfishness. We can unlearn our own deep conviction of our-selves as isolated, separate, and limited entities.

If we look at the experience that we call being alive and hon-estly see what the contents of consciousness are, we will see that we fail to bring our full attention to living. Because we are filled with desire, anger, loneliness, and fear, our conditioned self cannot stop comparing, wanting, defending, resenting, and being afraid. If we could bring our full attention and presence to each moment of life, that false, conditioned self would run out of energy.

This state of compulsive living is so painful, and its loneliness is so great, that we do everything we can to escape it through dreams of it being otherwise—through entertainments, through self-gratification, through seeking in spiritual circles the love that we do not feel for ourselves. If we could just be, we would be able to relax from the anxiety of becoming something that we are not, getting something we don't have, and trying to shape reality according to our own desires.

Too often we do not want to change, but instead want the pain to go away and allow us to remain the same with all our desires and with our image of ourselves intact. We will not be successful running to anything, because we cannot run away from ourselves. And yet what we most need is what we already are: our essential Self. There is no escape; there is only coming home.

When we really begin to see the state of our lives, we will also understand that we must turn most of our life around if we wish to be ourselves. It is our own personality that must be reoriented and developed in order that we may not be under the tyranny of our own false self. The ego is not to be discarded or demeaned; after it has been taken down from its commanding position it may become a useful servant. The personality can then be guided by an inner discrimination and can begin to act in response to the needs of the moment, not from compulsion or misguided self-interest. The submission of the lower self to the higher Self, of the self to the Whole in each moment becomes the central fact of existence. Submission is to live for one's Self—the eternal I—not for one's ego.

The Essential Self

What is this essential Self? How can we know whether we are in touch with it or whether we are engaged in wishful thinking? Does the essential Self have an objective reality, an ontological presence?

This is not the place to ask and answer every question about the existence of the human soul or the reality of the Unseen. Even assuming a certain level of spiritual awareness and sensitivity on the part of those who read this book, some questions are inevitable. Does the essential Self exist, or is it merely an effective notion to carry us beyond the limitations of the conventional mind?

Objective reality usually refers to things that we apprehend with our senses, whether they be objects, forces, or natural laws. Even an idea has a kind of existence, but if the idea contains an impossibility—as does the idea of a square circle, for instance—it exists *only* as an idea and refers to nothing real. Some might say that the essential Self is such an idea, that even the idea of a witnessing presence is a mere epiphenomenon, a byproduct, of certain physiological processes.

But what if we were to experience something more real than what we can see and touch, something more ourselves than our body, or our role in society, or our personal history—more real in fact than even our thoughts and emotions? Can this essential Self be experienced?

Whatever we can know is dependent on our state of consciousness. In the state of sleep, for instance, our knowing is limited to the functioning of the mind that we call dreaming. As long as we are in a state of sleep, we will interpret even sensory impressions—such as sounds and sensation—in terms of the dream we are experiencing. If a glass of water spills on the night table and drips onto us, we may dream that we are being drenched in the rain. Unless we wake up, even this sensory information will be shaped by the subjectivity of our sleeping dream.

In our so-called *waking* state we are open to sensory impressions in a more objective sense, and yet we may still distort what is happening before our very eyes. It is common for several people to witness exactly the same event and have very different ideas of what actually happened. The wise have been telling humanity that it is asleep even though it thinks it is awake. Muhammad said, "This life is a dream and when we die we awaken." Even this waking state can include a kind of dreamlike distortion.

Beyond the facts of sensory existence, or concurrent with this existence, is the dimension of qualities that are perceived by even subtler faculties than our senses. If we read great poetry with only our sensory mind and intellect, we may know the literal, concrete meanings of the words—we may know whether or not it makes sense on a concrete or intellectual level—but we will not necessarily know the meaning, feel the nuances, or catch the emotional taste of it. We may in one moment be reading poetry as mere words; but with a change of consciousness, with the heart open and engaged, the same lines might inexplicably bring tears to our eyes. What is it that controls this flow of tears? Why does this experience arise from our depths? What we experience is dependent on our state of consciousness.

The essential Self is an objective reality, but it cannot be known in a state of sleep, any more than the ordinary facts of reality can be known in a dream. In the Sufi tradition it is written that the absolute Spirit said, "And I breathed My Spirit into humanity." We are each enlivened by this inbreath. The essential Self, the soul, can be understood as this individualization of Spirit. The soul, however, is such a fine and subtle energy that it can be obscured by coarser energies of our existence, the energies of thought, desire, instinct, and sensation. These are the veils over the essential Self, the substances of intoxication that numb us to our essential Self.

If the essential Self, the soul, is engaged, it has the powers of Being, Doing, Living, Knowing, Speaking, Hearing, and Loving. From essential attributes like these proceed all the qualities that we need to live an abundant life. Within this nondimensional point of the essential Self (nondimensional because it has its existence in the realm of true Being, which appears to us as nonexistence) is the treasury of all qualities. We may receive what we need to be of service from this treasury through a process of conscious or unconscious activation, but it is our right as human beings to receive consciously. The human being is a channel for the creative power of the universe. Through the use of will—conscious choice—we can activate the qualities and powers of the essential Self.

Is the essential Self something that is veiled from the conscious mind and that can be known only indirectly, like Jung's unconscious? For Jung, the Self was an archetype of the wholeness of the unconscious. All our images of wholeness—including Divinity, Christ, and the Tao—represented this unconscious archetype, which would never be known directly. This reveals a fundamental truth of the essential Self—that it is infinite and can never be fully comprehended by consciousness alone—but it is only a partial truth, because, at the same time, we can see with the eyes of the essential Self, hear with its ears, act with its will, forgive with its forgiveness, and love with its love.

In classical Sufism the continuum from the false self to the essential Self has been described in seven stages. The word for self, *nafs,* is also equivalent to "soul."

1. *The self of compulsion* seeks satisfaction primarily in satisfying its selfish, carnal desires and its will to power. It is mentioned in the Surah Yusuf, verse 53, of the Qur'an as "the self impelled to evil."

2. *The self of conscience* has begun to discriminate between right and wrong, and can sometimes resist the temptation to evil and selfish actions. It is mentioned in the Surah Qiyyamah, verse 2: "I call to witness the self of conscience."

3. *The self of inspiration* is inspired with spiritual knowledge and can reliably follow the voice of conscience. It is mentioned in the Surah Shams, verses 7–8: "By the soul and the proportion and order given to it and its inspiration as to its right and its wrong." This is the highest stage that conventional religion and morality achieves.

4. *The soul of tranquility* has reached the level of presence in which a conscious intimacy is possible. It is described in Surah Fajr, verses 27–28: "O soul in tranquility, return to your Lord well-pleased and well-pleasing to Him."

5. *The soul of submission* has reached the level where its desires and actions are in harmony with Reality. It accepts each moment as it is and submits itself to Reality. This is described in Surah Ma'idah, verse 122: "Allah is well-pleased with them and they with God."

6. *The soul of total submission* is even more completely identified with the Universal Will. This is the stage of the great saints whose lives may be a profound and miraculous example of human wholeness. These people are lost in God.

7. *The soul of perfection* is a theoretical absolute, the perfected or complete human being as described in the Surah Shams, verse 9: "Truly he succeeds who purifies [the soul]."

Stages 1 and 2 are more or less under the domination of the false self. Stage 3 might be called the natural self, whereas stages 4 through 7 represent various degrees of the essential Self.

We can have no sense of the essential Self unless we arrive at our core—that which is deeper than thoughts and emotions, likes and dislikes, or opinions and ambitions. It is possible to listen within while following the rising of the breath, to listen for a silence behind thoughts and emotions. This silence is the background of what we normally pay attention to. Once this state is somewhat established we might direct our mind to our birth, to the mystery of our coming into the world. We can feel love for this being entering upon life. We might then focus on a funeral, our own. We might then bring the beginning and the end of our life into the present moment, viewing this present moment with the eyes of eternity, of our loving Creator. With this viewpoint, which is that of the essential Self, many wounds can be healed, many mistakes forgiven, and many losses accepted.

Rumi has also said in one of his odes (*Divani Shamsi Tabriz* #120):

Don't go, come near!
Don't be faithless, be faithful!
Find the antidote in the venom.
Come to the root of the root of your Self.

Molded of clay, yet kneaded
from the substance of certainty,
a guard at the Treasury of Holy Light—
come, return to the root of the root of your Self.

Once you get a hold of selflessness,
you'll be dragged from your ego,
and freed from many traps—
come, return to the root of the root of your Self.

You are born from the children of God's creation,
but you've fixed your sight too low.
How can you be happy?
Come, return to the root of the root of your Self.

Though you are a talisman protecting a treasure,
you are also the mine.
Open your hidden eyes
and come to the root of the root of your Self.

You were born from a ray of God's majesty
and have the blessings of a good star.
Why suffer at the hands of things that don't exist?
Come, return to the root of the root of your Self.

You came here from the presence of that fine Friend,
a little drunk, but gentle, stealing our hearts
with that look so full of fire, so
come, return to the root of the root of your Self.

Our master and host, Shamsi Tabriz,
has put the eternal cup before you.
Glory be to God, what a rare wine!
So come, return to the root of the root of your Self.

Befriending the Ego

Help me with this ego of mine
that is seeking help from You;
I seek justice from no one
but this justice-seeking self.
I shall not get justice from anyone
except Him who is nearer to me than myself;
for this I-ness comes moment by moment from Him.

RUMI, *MATHNAWI*, I, 2195–98

For many years my own focus within this Work was on conscious awareness and will. This moment-by-moment presence could be achieved by efforts to remember, to be conscious. I could see that without this discipline of conscious awareness we lived partly like animals, partly like machines, but not yet as human beings able to exercise choice, able to respond clearly to each moment rather than reacting from blind habit and expectation. I understood the Work as developing a sensitivity to the present by increasing awareness. Awareness did not develop automatically but through a clear intention formed by the will. To the extent that presence developed, it was through choice and effort. The ego might prefer to wallow in its compulsive and unconscious ways, but something within me could struggle with that.

Anyone who has worked for long enough in this way will eventually face a subtle but essential question: Can the ego be transformed by its own efforts? Is there the danger of merely being at war within ourselves, one part of the ego clashing with another, building up tension and frustration within us? Will this ever free us from the separate ego?

The sole tamer of the ego is love. We must learn to love even the ego; then the ego can submit to that love. Perhaps we need to consider what the ego is and how to live with it.

The ego is formed through trying to hold a place for ourselves in a world that has many contrary forces. As we grow into life, we face challenges and demands. We attempt to establish a position from which or through which to act. The ego is a fundamentally positive energy with many positive qualities: aspiration, diligence, responsibility, self-respect, discipline, and integrity.

These positive qualities can be seen as belonging to the Source and being reflected through us. As we develop these qualities, the positive aspect of ego, we will see how this ego is supported by a spiritual intelligence and wisdom, and how it can in return act as an instrument of this greater intelligence rather than as a proponent of its own self-interest. We need to establish a subtle balance—the ego in co-creatorship with the Spirit.

What is positive in us is much greater than what is negative. Whatever exists is essentially good. If there were not some good in it, it would not exist at all. Sometimes, however, these positive qualities can stand between us and Reality if they are appropriated by the ego's self-importance. The false self can ruin anything it touches. The tyrannical ego, which mercilessly drives us, needs to be brought down to its proper size and become a useful servant, messenger, and friend. We need the power of an integrated ego, but we need it as our servant, not as our master.

The only force that can effectively transform this tyrant comes through the essential Self. The only efforts that are effective are those supported by a greater wisdom within us. Transforming the ego is not just a struggle on one level, but an opening to a higher level: the choice of surrender, of submission to a greater will and intelligence. Submission is not an attribute of ego; we cannot say we are getting good at submission, the way that we can improve at most skills.

Submission, the true spiritual attitude, is being actively receptive to an intelligence that is greater than that of ourselves. It is an intention of gracefulness and surrender, of seeing the world as a stage, of seeing the Divine Unknown as the director. Submission has something to do with relaxing tensions, both superficial and deep. The only real relaxation is relaxation within Spirit.

The drama, however, is full of unexpected disappointments, tests, and frustrations. Just when we think we are reaching a point of trust, something comes up to disturb us, such as the negativity of other people, money problems, or health difficulties. Our first response sometimes creates tension within us, but we can discover a quality of submission to the necessity of what is. In other words, we can become actively receptive, and from there we can take appropriate action.

So often we foolishly expect outer life to be perfect. Yet the freedom, relaxation, and peace we are to find is not outer, but inner. Life on earth is a mixture of beauty and suffering. It is a challenging school—not the source of our comfort and security. Our home is in sanctity and love.

We exist in an environment where we must face the negative manifestations of other egos as well as those of our own. We pick up tension from our environment as well as producing it ourselves. It is essential to learn to relax within the tensions of life. We cannot escape conflict in this world, but we can learn to relax within it. This has nothing to do with running from conflict and certainly nothing to do with repressing it. This relaxation has aspects of trust, surrender, and submission. Balance is necessary. We need some tension in our lives to keep us from becoming complacent and without aspiration, but we also need to trust.

The Work exists to help us to remove all that separates us from Reality. These obstacles are the neurotic manifestations of ego that are produced by various kinds of physical, mental, and emotional tensions, whether aggressiveness, timidity, self-righteousness, self-doubt, arrogance, shame, hypocrisy, envy, jealousy, suspicion, or greed. In such states the ego will work overtime to maintain itself and its illusions.

Even for those who have chosen the Work of transformation, negative forces may sometimes come into consciousness with surprising force. This is a sign that a small, desperate part of ourselves is trying to perpetuate itself. Sensing that it is faced with its own annihilation or absorption into something greater but unknown, it will rebel against what seems to threaten it, not the least of which is real love, the brotherhood, the Work itself. This rebelliousness and its manifestations can be first recognized and observed, and then lovingly dissolved. We can be thankful for our faults, for they can keep us humble and aware of our dependence on a higher Reality, without which we would never be transformed.

As we refresh our spiritual intentions, as we cultivate patience, gratitude, humbleness, and love, we come to trust the Beneficence. In this process we will dissolve our deepest fears and tensions and they will be less of a motivating factor. With this dissolution of fear and tension the positive attributes of the ego—aspiration, diligence, responsibility, self-respect, discipline, and integrity—will emerge.

O, happy the soul that saw its own faults,
and if anyone mentioned a fault
wished eagerly to take responsibility—
for half of each person
has always belonged to the realm of fault,
but the other half belongs
to the Realm of the Unseen.

RUMI, *MATHNAWI*, II, 3034–35

Polishing the Mirror
of Awareness

There is a polish for everything,
and the polish for the heart is the remembrance
of God.

A SAYING OF THE PROPHET MUHAMMAD

Mevlana Jelaluddin Rumi said, "Let go of your worries and be completely clear hearted, like the face of a mirror that contains no images. When it is empty of forms, all forms are contained within it. No face would be ashamed to be so clear."

Rumi is reminding us that we can be clear-hearted only when we have polished the mirror. The mirror of awareness can become free of all images, especially images of ourselves. The spiritual process, practically speaking, can be understood as consciously polishing the mirror of awareness.

This mirror is like a sensitive screen on which appear our thoughts, desires, fears, expectations, and conditioning, and on which Spirit may also purely reflect. We have all heard the phrase "stream of consciousness," a vague and confusing expression, especially if we are concerned with distinguishing the stream from what floats in it. We should understand consciousness as the context and not the contents. Consciousness is sometimes used to mean the contents of awareness, as in "ecological consciousness." But we can intentionally distinguish the content of this awareness—that which is known in the mirror of awareness or perception—from the context, our sense of consciousness itself.

Only through being conscious, aware of the context of experience, can we discern what we habitually hold in our awareness. If human awareness is like a mirror, this mirror is normally filled with the contents of our sensory and psychological experience. Because it is so habitually filled with experience, and because our attention is so absorbed in these contents, the mirror of awareness itself is overlooked.

Actually, the mirror is only a partial metaphor for human awareness, because unlike a mirror, this awareness can reflect many levels of reality in addition to the physical—emotions, thoughts, and subtler perceptions such as intuition—and it can reflect these different levels selectively or simultaneously. There are many levels of Being, but each level participates in the One Being.

In meditation we learn to focus our attention on the sensitive screen of awareness, rather than becoming absorbed in its contents. Thoughts and feelings are the contents of the mirror, not the mirror itself. To the extent that we are collected and awake, we can see them as images in the mirror.

In addition to becoming familiar with our own thoughts and feeling states as if they were being reflected we also learn to clear the mirror, if only briefly. It is only by learning to clear it of its superficial contents that we can discover the deeper levels of ourselves in the mirror of the heart.

Each human being has the capacity to know many levels of experience. All the levels that are open to us, and these are much greater than is normally supposed, can be experienced in the mirror of human awareness. What is usually experienced in the mirror of human consciousness, however, is an accidental and unintentional assortment of personal compulsions and cultural conditioning.

This mirroring capacity is limited by the condition of the mirror. Its reflective capacity is reduced by the quantity and quality of our images, thoughts, and feelings, which accumulate upon the mirror. The mirror of pure awareness is obscured by layers of emotional and mental conditioning. Just as polishing transforms a mineral or stone into a reflective object, the human being who can regularly wipe clean the mirror of awareness will begin to reflect the light of Being itself. The spiritual process can be understood as learning to consciously reflect more and more of this Being.

If we could clear the inner mirror, the light of Being would be reflected outwardly as light, as light pouring out of our eyes.

In polishing the mirror of the heart, the most obvious level of rust contains our compulsions and negative feeling states—the demands of ego. We must first recognize, respect, and surrender these negative states. We release them by recognizing them, and each surrender is a little death. Through this process of letting go with each breath, we can become free of the compulsive mind, to experience a new freedom, with a new depth and a new height.

One of the first things to observe is the continuous presence of like and dislike, the grinding clash of opposites. We are continually preferring one thing to another, and this leads to anxiety and resentment in different degrees. We are normally so absorbed with our likes and dislikes, desires and frustrated desires that we rarely notice or question them, and so we remain in unconscious slavery. In such a state we fail to be open and to see because we are so consumed with the contents of the mirror. We are veiled from our spiritual intentions, from our magnetic center, by needs and rationalizations, by self-justification and compulsion, by the tyranny of the sleeping personality.

For example, sometimes the mirror of awareness is obscured

by a compulsive neediness. There are people who are compelled to constantly seek attention from others. At every opportunity, in order to hold another's attention, they tell people about their problems, their experiences, and their opinions. In such a state, preoccupied with the compulsive neediness of their personality, they are not receptive to what the wider reality offers. Their mirror is obscured by this overwhelming need to receive attention.

Sometimes unconscious needs obscure the mirror that would give us objective perceptions. Consider someone who is strongly attracted by a certain look in the opposite sex—a certain slant of the eyebrow or shape of the nose—and because of this is blind to the most obvious personality flaws in the possessor of this attractive physical feature.

The ego is ruled by personal desire. The ego thrives on like and dislike, and on comparison. It prefers what it imagines will guarantee its satisfaction and security. It thus produces an endless succession of desires and dislikes—a repertoire of emotions such an envy, greed, resentment, self-importance, and self-pity. Because the ego is completely preoccupied with itself—with its concepts, opinions, and emotions, and with its gratification—it shuts itself off from the spiritual worlds and from greater Being.

The ego does not know it is asleep. It judges everything from its own perspective. It has created an imaginary world apart from the real world.

To discover the different levels on which this polishing needs to occur, and how might the mirror itself be polished, we need to pass over the threshold between our society's distorted norms and that unknown territory that is the soul's true land.

In our own times, our mirrors are layered by images of the commercial world: hardly any place on earth is free of the pollution of advertising and commercial entertainment. This is society's means of hypnotizing and enslaving us. Can any soul discover itself when filled with preoccupations of that commercial culture?

In the psychological domain, psychic material (thoughts, emotions, likes, and dislikes) can obscure the mirror. A compulsive thought—a criticism, for instance, repeated unconsciously—can contribute to an accumulation of conditioning. Unexamined likes and dislikes layer the heart with expectation. Even pleasant emotions, such as fascination, can be a veil over the heart. We need a free, discriminating attention and wakefulness.

If we periodically examine the quality of our thoughts, our own inner preoccupations, we will begin to know ourselves as we are. We can regularly ask ourselves: What is our inner life really like? How much are we controlled by ambition, secrecy, hypocrisy, and distorting desire? Without indulging either in guilt or in mindless innocence, we can use the Work to purify the inner self of conditioning, negativity, and hypocrisy, in order to be able to act more purely, authentically, and spontaneously. The Work is to bring the outer and the inner into harmony.

On the level of relationships and ethics, all compulsive relationships, manipulations of others, and actions that lead to greater separateness will obscure the mirror. Our heedlessness and thoughtlessness in ethical matters and human relationships will trap and entangle us. All our relationships should be governed by conscious reflection and a sensitive heart. These are the keys to conscience.

In the material world our activity can more or less reflect order and harmony. This requires attention to our intention. If our intention is clear and sound, and if it is periodically remembered and reaffirmed, there will be a mental, emotional, and practical integration in realizing the intention. Haste, carelessness, and distraction will be lessened. We all have tasks and functions to fulfill—ethically, psychologically, and spiritually. Polishing the mirror of awareness increases the clarity of our relationship to each task before us.

As we approach what might be called the sane human state—freer of the compulsive ego—we begin to see more clearly that even our thoughts are dust upon the mirror. When we have come to know Being, we see that it is vaster and wider than the space previously occupied by thinking alone. Actually, thoughts themselves are not a problem any more than are sense perceptions, such as vision, hearing, or tasting. If we learn to be present to all these impressions, if we are conscious, if we are gathered to our own "I," we are increasing a Divine presence in the world. The important thing is not to let these impressions erase our presence, but to attempt to remember with each breath, to remain aligned with Being.

Is this asking the impossible? Can we polish the thoughts from the mirror and become this simple presence? Can we be so reflective that our thoughts reflect this clarity and light?

It is the work of presence to connect the separate parts, the different levels—from the physical energies, through the sensitive and conscious energies, to the levels of creative, cosmic, and unitive energies. There are many worlds: the mineral world, the world of nature, the business world, the mental and emotional worlds, the world of creativity, the spiritual world, and the world of union.

The great prophets have come to remind humanity of the real world, the unity between the parts and the Whole, the unity of all these different levels that enables a spark of love on the highest level to create and manifest so much on other levels. The prophets have also come to warn of the effects of actions that are not in harmony with this real world. To be fully human, the prophets have said, is to live consciously, in the presence of the Divine on many levels of Being. If we cut ourselves off from this Whole, if we lose respect and love for the One, we fall into fragmentation and conflict.

Our false sense of separation and our consequent slavery to like and dislike veil us from this real world. This world and worldliness are based on a false separation. We can choose illusion or reality, depending on whether we decide to polish our mirrors.

In the world of the Spirit, the human being is a witness. The mirror is for witnessing not only the outer, visible world but the inner, invisible worlds where spiritual qualities dwell. Through the sensitive screen of our own awareness, we behold moment by moment and flash by flash the manifestation of infinite beauty, and that beauty need never be absent from the mirror. What may appear in the mirror at a given moment is a gift and should never be underestimated or taken for granted. As we polish away conditioning, concepts, and the false, reacting self, wherever we turn there is the face of Reality. "There is a polish for everything," said Muhammad, peace and blessings upon him, "and the polish for the heart is the remembrance of God."

Listening Within

Since in order to speak, one must first listen,
learn to speak by listening.

RUMI, *MATHNAWI*, I, 1627

It is possible to restructure the brain so that there is more conscious awareness. This has been called polishing the mirror, awakening from sleep, cultivating the witness, and developing the real "I." Through changing the energy level of the brain, we can activate a different kind of brain function—a finer attention that stands above routine, habitual thought, feeling, and behavior.

This presence—this conscious, listening mind—not only opens a window on our experience, it also connects us to the source of will. Attention can be called the first act of the will. It establishes the relationship between observer and experience, raising the level of experience and transforming a living automaton into a sensitive agent. It is this sensitivity that makes the difference between being nominally awake and experiencing life as the gift it is.

Almost everyone has some area of his or her life in which some sensitive awareness is developed. Some people find it in painting, some in playing softball, others in meeting people, and still others in religious worship. But few people manage to sustain the fresh edge of sensitive awareness through the circumstances of their daily life. Instead they settle for routines and habits.

A change in energy level occurs when we move from passive to active attention. When our attention is passive, we are reacting to random stimuli from the environment and from within our own psychology. We are weakened and fragmented by the various demands that occupy our attention.

An active attention, on the other hand, allows us to be receptive and whole by connecting us to a willing "I," a more unified and harmonized presence. This active attention, which originates in the will, creates more and more energy of its own kind and brings increasing freedom from the processes within the mind. It allows us to listen in on our thoughts more clearly and to feel our feelings. It is the beginning of knowing ourselves.

Through this process we are freed from the servitude to habitual thoughts and feelings. Many unconscious motivators—such as envy, resentment, and fear—lose some of their power over us. We are taken out of the darkness and brought into the light of awareness, where emotional contradictions can be seen and resolved, and self-defeating thought patterns can be understood and worked with.

This listening to our inner talking should first be practiced within the context of meditation, where it can be experienced under relatively controlled conditions. Listening to our thoughts is different from commenting on them. Conscious listening is possible only in a heightened awareness. The inner commentaries with which we are filled are an example of thought judging thought, one part of the intellectual mind commenting on another. This occurs normally in our everyday experience and is simply the result of our mind being made up of many separate parts, each having its opinions and judgments of the others. Conscious listening takes place on a different level, a viewpoint from which thinking, feeling, and behaving can be observed. If we practice this listening when we are quiet and still, focused only on the task of listening, we will see how we move from being identified with the process of thinking to being aware and relatively free of thought. Occasionally we have a moment of observing the process of thought itself.

Once we have practiced it enough to know it, we can attempt to introduce more of this listening into the midst of life. Occasionally we will catch ourselves at the end of a process of thinking and will awaken from it in much the same as we awaken from a dream. So much of our waking time is spent unconsciously identified with the process of thinking, out of touch with the present moment and situation, living in our heads.

If we have cultivated the observer in ourselves, we will notice times when our mental processes are not functioning creatively or harmoniously. This observer can begin to see when we carry resentment in the form of habitual complaints, when we indulge in self-pity or self-judgment, or when we play old tapes with negative themes.

If we observe our inner talking, we will see that each day our thoughts cluster around a few different themes. An event, a conversation, or some reading will set off reverberations in the mind. Some difficult situation will echo in our thoughts with surprising persistence, and these echoes will distort or at least color other experiences that have nothing to do with that past experience. This is one way that we carry the past inappropriately into the present. An unpleasant experience at work will be brought home. Difficulty with a family member might reflect on relationships outside the family. A certain pattern of thinking activated in one situation persists into another, making it more difficult to know the moment as it is.

If we are preoccupied with some worry, for instance, it absorbs most of our awareness. To the extent of this preoccupa-

Recuerdo del 472 Aniversario
de las Apariciones de la
Virgen de Guadalupe

M i corazón en amarte

eternamente se ocupe

y mi lengua en alabarte

M adre mía de Guadalupe

Asociación de la Virgen de Guadalupe
Parroquia de San Juan Bautista,
Coyoacán, D.F.
Diciembre 12 de 2003
Fray Fernando Parra, OFM
Párroco

tion, this absorption of awareness, we are absent from the present moment. Imagine, for instance, that while at work I received news of some unexpected expense and I am worried about paying it. As I drive home my thoughts echo this preoccupation. I drive unconsciously, automatically. I carry this preoccupation into my home and perhaps seem distant to others around me, not really enjoying their company or giving them my real attention. Depending on the degree of my self-awareness, I may not really be conscious of the time I have lost, nor of what is occupying my thinking. In other words, much of this may be happening on an unconscious level. Not only is the present moment obscured, but the contents of my own mind may not be known because my "I" is so absorbed in what is going on. In this state of identification with mechanical talking almost nothing is possible for me.

But not all of our inner dialog is useless or negative. The mind seems to need some of this free associating and automatic processing in order to digest experience, to consider alternative behaviors, and to receive suggestions from the unconscious. This somewhat unconscious functioning of the mind is quite productive when we are involved in solving problems, asking real questions, or focusing ourselves through creative effort. In most creative processes, from art to engineering, there is a phase of looking clearly at what there is, asking what is needed, formulating the question or clarifying the intention—in other words, doing all the necessary homework—and then letting go, even forgetting about the whole thing. This is when the subconscious mind can do its hidden, most creative work.

What is the place of the witness or observer in this process? Perhaps it is at the stage of framing a question or an intention, especially in those moments when it is necessary to stand apart patiently to see the situation and consciously ask what is needed. After the homework is properly done, the observer need only check in now and then to see that the process is continuing in the direction of the original question or intention. When we live with a real question and a sense of purpose, the whole mind is more likely to function harmoniously and creatively.

More and more we will also begin to have experiences of pure presence free of thought. Opening to life without preconception, without the veil of habitual thought, we will perceive Being. Our brains have been programmed through evolution to perceive differences. Being is fundamentally changeless and eternal, and therefore quite easy for the brain to ignore. But we can train our attention to perceive Being at the same time that it perceives change and differences. If we learn to include this awareness of Being, we will be living more fully in the present moment. Against the background of this Being or Presence, our preoccupations and obsessions will become clearer to us and we will be able to work with them better, provided we have the knowledge and willingness to do so.

As a certain psychological space opens up within us through conscious presence, we begin to live differently. Thought, instead of being a largely unconscious process absorbing our awareness and presence, becomes creative and effective. It recognizes possibilities and builds images. Thought opens channels, connects human hearts, and heals. As an attribute of the essence, thought completes the connection between the invisible world of possibility and the manifest world of forms.

If we are to take advantage of our life while we have this physical body, we will learn to use thought consciously rather than being used by it. We will find something in ourselves that transcends thought and make friends with it. We will be living more and more in a world of Spirit.

These simple exercises of self-observation are contributing to the development of another quality of Being within us, a state of true self-awareness and identification with Spirit.

The Dance
of Personality

The Sufi's book is not of ink and letters;
it is nothing but a heart white as snow.

RUMI, *MATHNAWI*, II, 159

The human mind has two main facets: one, a limited awareness, which includes intellect, emotions, and perception; and the other, the subconscious, which encompasses many faculties within a much greater domain. The mind's limited department, the lower self, is governed by reason and desire; its infinite, subconscious department, the higher self, is spontaneously in communication with the mind of the universe.

The lower self can be understood to include intellect, emotions, and the sense of self they produce, the ego. The personality is just one aspect of this lower self.

Personality includes all our learned behavior—our likes and dislikes, our ways of expressing ourselves—as distinct from our innate, inherited capacities. Personality is a product of conditioning and education. We even learn our negative emotions through imitation, which is why so-called civilized and cultured people can sometimes display an extensive repertoire of negative behavior and emotions. More *primitive* people, those from simpler, traditional societies, are relatively uncomplicated in both their happiness and their disappointment.

Personality is something we develop to relate to our environment. I *am* a soul, an awareness, and I *have* a body, and I also have a personality. Like the body, we need it to get around in this world. Personality is the acquired and artificial complex of habits of relating to other human beings. We relate to other people through certain roles, and there is a tendency for the role to take over. As we learn to observe ourselves and others, we see how we virtually click into different roles, becoming different people depending on whom we are with and what situation we are in. One person is meek and reticent in a spiritual group, but with a little to drink and some music is ready to unclothe and dance on a table-top. Another person shows great warmth and friendliness with strangers, but is sullen and withdrawn in more intimate relationships. And still another is ruthless and impersonal in the business world, but is sweet and indulgent with a pet cat.

Each of us is a package of subpersonalities. We more or less unconsciously play different roles depending on whom we are with, whether we trust the other person, whether we want something, and whether we wish to impress or be accepted. We identify with these different personalities. We lose ourselves and our awareness in them. Often because we feel the need to protect ourselves and avoid conflict, we use personality—with all its social conventions and subtle lying—to slide over potential problems. As civilized and educated people we have acquired much personality in the form of manners and conventions, do's and don'ts, and layers of social programming. Because we spend so much time relating to other human beings with this acquired personality, we forget what a real relationship can be. For instance, when we are under pressure and are pushing to get things done, we can see other human beings as obstacles in our way. And yet when we relate to other people as objects, we ourselves become machines with automatic routines and programs.

We need not wear our hearts on our sleeves or insist that complete openness in society is always desirable. The deeper levels of the heart can be shared only when there is a certain trust, and openness is not always appropriate. The heart needs a doorkeeper, and this too is the function of a discriminating personality.

Some people delight in the play of their personalities—in the interaction of their social self with another's. If this play develops out of that in ourselves which is conscious, it can be full of life, joy, and humor. But if it is only the interaction of shells, what real human contact is there? Is personality, itself, a form of aliveness, or is it a form of habit and mechanicality? Can we ever escape some form of personality in our relationships? Isn't the most important fact whether the personality manifests spirit rather than smothering it?

If personality is an unexamined and unconscious habit that governs our relationships, the life and spirit within us is choked off. We become robots with a limited set of experiences, even if some of these experiences are exciting. But, as we awaken the soul, the observer in ourselves, we can begin to notice the habits and qualities of our personality. Unfortunately, as soon as we meet another in relationship, our presence often disappears and the habits of our personality take over. But in those moments in which we catch a glimpse of ourselves, particularly in a relationship, we can begin to feel what is real and connected with our Essence and what is more artificial. Has my personality developed out of too much self-importance, or is it restricted by low self-esteem? Do I take myself too seriously, or do I habitually underestimate myself? Do I wear a mask of aloofness, or do I enter all relationships with an abnormal level of excitement? We can sense these unconscious aspects of personality only from another viewpoint, a viewpoint that lies behind the facade of personality.

We would do well to ask ourselves about the origins of our behavior. Does it come from the mechanical habits of the personality, or is it spontaneously guided by the heart?

The study of the personality is the study of the lower self. Perhaps there are rare individuals who are brought up in an ideal environment with mature and enlightened parents—people who have had a chance to develop a balanced personality shaped by friendliness, openness, trust, generosity, patience, and other Essence qualities. But what about the vast majority who have a share of insecurity, suspicion, envy, selfishness, and impatience?

So much of our work is with the lower self, the ego and intellect, including the personality. We don't need to work on the higher Self; there is nothing to do with this Self other than make contact with it, listen to it, and become aware of its guidance. It is the personality that needs help and training, but it can be trained only by the higher Self. With awareness I can use and direct what I have. Like a painter I can increase the colors on my palette. What colors I choose to use depend on the needs of the moment. The soul—which is a ray of Spirit, and carries the attributes of awareness, love, and will—can direct the personality.

Personality can be a servant of the soul, or it can cause the soul to shrink back into insignificance. We can live life from our Essence awareness with the personality as a vehicle, or we can live it from the personality's social programming alone—which means relating to life superficially and mechanically.

The personality can be either a means of binding us together in solidarity with other human beings or a means of separating us from others through its habits of rudeness, exclusivity, superficiality, comparison, and judgment. We can be the kind of people who harmonize with others and bring them into productive relationships, or we can be divisive, exclusive, envious, competitive, and suspicious, labeling people as "other," seeing them as objects.

The example of human beings who realized their unity with Spirit can provide a model of behavior and conduct by which one may be assured of moral security and spiritual health.

Jesus, peace and blessings upon him, said, "The gentle [not the "meek"] will inherit the earth." The Greek word for *gentle* also has the meaning of "well-trained." It is useful for us to examine and observe the impulses of the personality, the compulsive ego, in our relationships. We must see how this results in disharmony and observe our inner states at the moment of action. Harmony is possible when we empty ourselves of ourselves.

Muhammad, peace and blessings upon him, said, "I came to perfect moral virtues." The example of his speech and actions, conscientiously noted and preserved, remains as a lasting model for a large percentage of humanity. Each human being, to the extent of his or her ignorance, faces danger, insecurity, alienation, and disease. In this world we do not escape the lawful consequences of our actions. Just as we will get sick if we eat food that is not healthy, so too speech and actions will have their consequences. It is useful to remember another saying of Muhammad: "God gives a high rank to him who is gentle in everything."

We don't have to look very far to see examples of the anarchy of ignorance. To the extent that human behavior originates from egoism, selfishness, greed, fear, and lying, relationships are chaotic, individuals are alienated, and society itself is unhealthy.

Interdependence is a living practice. Courtesy, manners, and right action are the expressions of a practice that allows brotherhood to find expression. It is most characteristic of the Way of Love.

This practice begins with respect. We can respect the carpet that is walked on, the cup that is drunk from, the candle that bears light. In times past a dervish wouldn't "put out" a candle; he would "put it to rest." A dervish, knowing that the world *dervish* also means "threshold," always paused in remembrance before stepping over the threshold. In this respect for inanimate things is the recognition of an identity between the observer and what is observed. Although the material world is not taken as the final reality, it is considered a manifestation of Spirit and therefore worthy of respect.

If the material world deserves our gratitude and respect, if the Sufis kiss the tea glass from which they drink, how much more respect do they owe to other creatures and beings? There is a story about Hazrati Ali, the close companion of Muhammad, who was once late for the dawn prayer. The prophet, who was leading the prayer, was about to begin when the Angel Gabriel appeared and asked him to wait a little while longer. At that moment, Ali was on his way to the mosque, but he had found himself walking behind an old Jewish man. Out of respect for this man's age Ali did not want to pass him on the street. Because of this respect, Allah, who did not want Ali to miss the benefit of the first prostration of the day, sent Gabriel to delay the beginning of prayers.

It has been said by Muhammad, "Humility is the foremost act of worship." Inner selflessness manifests itself in one's actions. In traditional circles students don't turn their backs to a teacher, leader, or other respected person, and they do not stick their feet out directly toward another person. A thoughtful person offers a seat to any guest or older person and considers their comfort first. On this esoteric path there are certain manners to be observed, never as mere formality, but in remembrance of this fundamental respect.

The personality can either serve as the reflecting lamp of our Essence—magnifying or focusing the light of the soul—or be the bushel that hides that light. Every human being carries a seed of the Essence that is meant to be actualized. This Essence has no limits. Limits are imposed only by the condition of the vehicle that carries it.

Gathering the
Fragmented Self

With will, fire becomes sweet water;
and without will, even water becomes fire.
RUMI, *MATHNAWI*, I, 1336

The experience of one's own identity, or "I," is a source of wonder from the first self-awareness of childhood through the whole of one's life. Each "I" seems unique and has its own personal history. The greatest variable in human nature is the characteristic quality of this "I" feeling. For some this feeling is one of alienation; for others it is one of communion with life. For some the feeling is one of self-deprecation; for others it may be one of profound self-worth. The "I" is a prison bounded by habitual thoughts and feelings for some; for others it is a hidden treasure.

Spiritual attainment is a fundamental transformation of the "I" from a separate, limited, and contracted identity into a rich and infinite one. It is a movement from separation to union.

One of the first steps in this process is to observe and understand the chaotic and fragmented nature of the ordinary self and to understand that a very practical integration and harmony can be achieved. This integrated self is the drop that contains the ocean. At the dimensionless center of our identity is the creative potential of Cosmic Mind.

FRAGMENTATION

We are forever in parts and yet wish to be whole. We are distracted and yet wish to concentrate; we are scattered and yet wish to be gathered.

We are scattered to the extent that we yield our "I" to every impulse. We say "my" likes or dislikes, "my" feelings, and "my" pain, and we diminish that "I" to the proportions of our personal pain. This "I" becomes enfeebled and is absorbed in all these things. At one time it is absorbed in a compulsive, unconscious act, at another in a vague anxiety. From one moment to the next, it moves through likes and dislikes, through various motives and preoccupations. Its attention quickly shifts from being occupied with what is in front of it to entering a daydream. Some sense of "I" is identified with each of these events.

We are fragmented when we wander from our own center. When our attention is merely reacting to outer events, or when it is being dominated by something, it loses contact with its own source. Attention is a sacred faculty, but when it is drawn to whatever pulls strongest, it has no force of its own; it is passive. If attention is not connected to will, a human is not fully a human being.

WHAT CAN YOU DO WITH WILL
THAT YOU CAN'T DO WITHOUT IT?

I have a friend who used to be the kind of person who was reliably unreliable. If he called and said he was coming to visit on Tuesday at eight, the one thing you could be sure of is that he wouldn't be there then. Just as every decision consciously completed brings will, every decision neglected costs will. Little by little one's life seems to be controlled by a negative chaos—a chaos of disorder, accident, sickness, debt, failure, missed opportunities, and so forth. To all of this one might assign the word freedom. *In one sense, he was the freest person that I knew; he went wherever the wind blew. From another point of view he was a slave to impulse. He once asked me, "What can you do with will that you can't do without it?" At the moment, standing next to his painted VW bus, I had no answer for him. A day later the answer came simple and clear: Be free.*

If we lose contact with our intention, we lose our own coherence; our actions are inconsistent with our feelings. Feelings or motivations that once supported our goals abandon us, leaving us helpless and unresolved. All transient pleasures come to their inevitable end, and all good intentions face continuous assaults. Life seems a continuous struggle, requiring a certain amount of effort just to keep up. The struggle of life is largely a struggle to get organized, to gather together a certain coherence within ourselves.

The distractions and demands of outer life can diminish our presence. If we are continually reacting to outside influences, we have little strength left for the inner life. Because we have been dispersed, we need to be gathered. Because we have been fragmented, we need to become whole, to collect ourselves and thereby let our light be stronger. No one can transform the ego before the ego has become integrated.

Prayer can be understood as the gathering of attention. The inner effort, which is the work of gathering and recollection, leads to peace within. When this peace has gathered sufficient strength it can face the world in a new way.

GATHERING

The experience of being gathered or mobilized seems to come from outside the parade of temporal events. It penetrates our conditioned world as the momentary experience of wholeness. It shows itself to be composed of our mental, emotional, and physical energies operating in a unified way in the present moment. When we are gathered there is a congruency in our behavior—in our body language, our speech, and our emotional tone. We are not projecting incongruity or sending multiple messages. The will is not fragmented.

We learn that awareness of our breath and physical presence can greatly assist this gathering. And we learn that to be identified with any single function, such as thinking or feeling, is to be without an "I Am"—without presence.

The essential matter here is that the human being is made up of many functions: sensory, behavioral, emotional, intellectual, psychic, and intuitive. When we live at the energy level of functioning automatons, those parts function in mechanical and habitual ways. At the level of sensitive energy, most of our attention is absorbed in just one function. We may be aware of thinking, or feeling, or sensing, but there is no overall awareness.

The secret to developing an integrated self is to intentionally extend awareness to more than one function at a time. Each function that comes into awareness adds another coordinate to our conscious existence. If, for instance, we are fully occupied with an emotion and become aware of our breathing, or our physical sensations, we have generated more presence. If those of us who live mostly in our heads, in repetitive and limited thinking, both add an awareness of something physical such as our breathing and come into touch with our feelings, we have extended our presence greatly. We have more coordinates. Instead of a one-dimensional person we have suddenly become a three- or four-dimensional person.

A pyramid whose base has thinking, feeling, and sensory awareness as its corners and conscious presence (on another level) as its apex is a useful model of the integrated self. All the functions of one level are integrated by this apex, and our wholeness depends on it. The most practical capacity as well as the deepest aspect of worship depends on this wholeness. In practical life we develop a mastery given to us by the very presence of an "I"; in worship we enter the presence of Spirit with loving respect and awe.

Some higher, harmonizing force is responsible when all our parts are brought together. Sometimes this harmonizing force may be produced by circumstances, as when a strong emotion temporarily integrates us. But if we can increase our ability to intentionally integrate all our parts into a unified whole, we will be masters of ourselves rather than slaves of ego. If we can gather ourselves to that nondimensional point of our own identity, everything will be subordinated to this point, this "I." As this "I," this capacity for presence, develops, it becomes our connection to Infinite Life.

There are two practical currents in the process of gathering and mobilizing the mind: an inner movement and an outer one.

Because we have been dispersed in things, including thoughts and feelings, we can first gather ourselves inwardly to the core of ourselves, to that dimensionless point. So the first step is to gather all attention, awareness, and will toward that nondimensional point of contact with Spirit and listen within. We can come to this point only in nakedness and ignorance, leaving behind all thought, accomplishment, and power. Otherwise our attention will be dispersed in all these things.

Having directed our attention toward our essence in meditation, we are rejuvenated from within ourselves. It is not necessary to have direction or intention in meditation, beyond the intention to be gathered, but sooner or later we face the necessity of action. It is only after creating an inner vacuum that we can again turn outward with the fullness of presence.

Collectedness carried into action can include a degree of intention. We may begin in the awareness of stillness, but if we wish to extend that awareness we must decide on some purposeful activity for ourselves. Both the decision and the act of carrying it out are the fruit of this gathering/mobilizing. We can learn to gather and mobilize all that is within our awareness.

In this bringing together, all outer things are reminders of Being itself: Wherever you look is the face of the Friend. Eventually this process can become circular—presence welling up inside us and moving outward, the outer world being consciously recognized and returned back to its source through our awareness. We live for Spirit and Spirit sustains us.

CHOPPING WOOD

During my early years in the Work, on one of the rare occasions when I was able to spend some time at the house of my teacher's teacher, some other men and I had been chopping wood not far from a small pond. The master had been observing some golden carp that had grown to great size. He walked slowly with a cane, still a striking figure in his eighties, with a clean-shaven head and a black patch over an eye that had been lost long ago. These fish would swim from the depths to the shallows, especially if you dropped them something to eat.

"When I observe my mind," I said, "what I mostly see are strange and unknown thoughts that come to the surface and disappear again. I have little control over what they are."

"This observation should be maintained," the master said, "but there is something more that you can do. You can gather positive thought and direct it anywhere you like. You can, for instance, visualize people who need your positive thought and simply direct it to them." My receptivity to what he was offering was so complete that I had no further questions or comments.

Later I was chopping a particularly stubborn piece of wood, a piece of elm that had been given to me by one of the older men, expecting, I suppose, that I wouldn't know that elm can be split only with great difficulty. I had struck it once and with great effort had pulled the ax out of the gnarled grain that held it ever more tightly the deeper I struck. The master approached us and said quietly, "Here is an example of what we were talking about. You have struck the wood once. Can you gather your mind and put the ax exactly into the first cut? Try now."

I gathered myself and swung. It came down a half-inch to the right of the first cut.

"Try again."

I did and the ax came down a half-inch to the left.

"Well," he said, "it has been a long time since I swung an ax, but let me have it." When he handed his cane to one of us, we were almost surprised he could stand without it. He swung the ax and it struck the wood.

"Now pull it out," he said.

When I pulled it out, there were only the three cuts.

The ax appeared to have struck the center cut exactly. "Now you try again—but with enough strength to split it."

I took the ax from him, and with a clarity and confidence that had never been my own, I swung the ax right through the elm, leaving the two halves on the ground.

Mysteries of the Body

We are bees, and our bodies are the honeycomb:
we have made the body, cell by cell, like beeswax.
RUMI, *MATHNAWI*, I, 1813

What is the significance of being embodied? And what is it that is embodied?

Having overcome the mind/body dualism, the very strange conception that mind and body have little to do with each other, we are aware that our emotions and thoughts can influence our state of mind. I need to take care of the mind, just as I need to take care of the body, but what is this "I" that takes care?

On the one hand, here "I" am; on the other hand everything—including this "I"—is a manifestation of the One Energizer of All Life. To say that there is no self is only as true as saying there is no car, no flower, or no "earth." All these phenomena are aspects of this wholeness. Something exists that is individualized, and yet this individualization is somehow integral to the whole. Am I the drop or the ocean? Both. I am the drop that contains the ocean and the drop that can merge with the ocean and, at will, be the drop again.

My teacher would say, "You *are* a soul, and you *have* a body." It is not the personality that has the body, but the transcendent intelligence that has a body, a personality, and a mind. It is the soul that can harmonize the bodymind.

The body is formed by the creative and energizing power of Life out of the substances of this earth. It has arisen out of the lands and seas of this earth. It is recycled material. The soul makes use of this bodymind. Through the beneficence of the Source of Life, we can touch, smell, hear, see, and feel. We can grasp the beauty and meaning of being lovers on this earth. Our bodies allow us to come into contact with one another. It is as beautiful for a child to take a grandparent's hand as it is for a young man to feel a young woman's breast. It is beautiful to embrace and feel the life in another body. It is beautiful to kneel and kiss the ground in worship.

Sometimes, however, we are enslaved to our bodies just as we can be enslaved to our egos. This is because the body is the generator of desire and, therefore, the generator of egoism and separation.

The body has been feared in many man-made belief systems, but no prophet ever denigrated it. Buddha advocated the Middle Way between asceticism and indulgence. Jesus washed the feet of his students! Muhammad said, "Your body has rights over you." But subsequent people invented belief systems of their own that punished and weakened the body, rather than strengthening the soul.

Today, in reaction to this history of repression, there is some tendency toward a regression to the body, as if the full expression of the soul will emerge by manipulating the body. Perhaps the new body therapies can provide a corrective to the repression of the body that Western culture has allowed, but the awakened soul cannot be reduced to bodily well-being, nor is the intelligence of the body, no matter how exquisite, the whole of intelligence.

Spirit loves the body. But when the bodymind eclipses the soul, neither body nor soul is happy. It is certainly a challenge to find the right relationship to the bodymind, just as it is a challenge to ride a spirited horse. Horse and rider can have a relationship in which the horse's spirited essence is developed and expressed. If there were no riders, horses would roam in wild unconscious herds; but because of the rider's love of the horse, a conscious relationship can develop that benefits both. The body, too, can benefit from the loving awareness of the soul; this awareness will not repress the spirit and intelligence of the body but guide it to fuller expression.

Bringing attention to a sense of our bodiliness, or sensing, is a means by which we can use the body to lead us to greater presence. When the energy of consciousness is blended with the energy of the body, the whole organism is spiritualized, raised to another level of experience. The practice of sensing, sustaining presence in the body, allows emotions to be more harmonious and thoughts less obsessive.

The powerfully positive effects of many diverse systems of bodywork can be traced back to this simple practice of sensate awareness, of blending conscious energy with the energies of the body. Sensing brings Spirit into the organism.

I know of a newspaper publisher who visited Russia and witnessed Orthodox Christian worshippers prostrating endlessly. From one point of view this practice might be seen as an abasement of the human body; yet from another point of view it is a way of praying with the whole body. As a New England Protestant he had experienced little to prepare him for the impressions that this prayer of the body made on him. It touched his soul so deeply that he gave up his publishing career and entered a seminary.

The martial arts of the Far East, such as Aikido and Tai Chi Chuan; sacred dances of all kinds, especially the whirling of the Mevlevi Sufis and the movements taught by Gurdjieff; ritual prayer, such as the Islamic Salaat—all consciously respect, integrate, and develop the body. All of these sacred means use the body as a medium for the expression of the creative powers of the soul. Furthermore, they produce an integration of all the faculties: not only the physical, but the emotional, the mental, and the spiritual.

The martial arts of the Far East teach a presence of mind through balance and alertness. You cannot delude yourself about being present when you have a physical opponent putting you to the test. If you daydream, you will find yourself an instant victim. These disciplines train the consciousness as much as the body.

The whirling of the Mevlevis requires physical precision and groundedness. The left foot never leaves the ground; the right foot repeats an exacting movement that allows the turner to move with extraordinary grace, neither wobbling nor bobbing up and down. While seeing the physical world turn around his own still axis, the *semazen* is inwardly repeating the name of God with each revolution. The arms are extended, an expression of longing and submission—the right palm up receiving spiritual energy, the left palm down bestowing that energy to the world. The *semazen* becomes a transformer of cosmic energies through conscious intention, love, and the electrodynamic effect of the human nervous system revolving in relation to the earth's magnetic field.

The movements that Gurdjieff brought from Sufi and other sources in Central Asia cannot be performed through thinking, but only by allowing a deeper moving intelligence to take over. They communicate a sense of the sacred, and yet they are like tongue-twisters for the body. By bringing the body into sequences of gesture and posture beyond conventional habits of movement, they activate the nervous system beyond its habitual structure of experience.

The Islamic ritual prayer, practiced five times a day, is a sequence of standing, bowing, prostrating, and kneeling, accompanied by prescribed verbal affirmations and lines from the Qur'an selected and recited by the individual. The prayer is understood to be invalid without a mindful witnessing of the presence of God. Physically, it exercises the major joints (especially the spinal column), massages the intestinal tract, transmits a reflex to the liver, regulates the breath, and stimulates the frontal cortex of the brain as it is brought low to the ground, while momentarily leaving the heart in a higher position than the brain. Salaat is a form that integrates mindfulness, mental precision, affirmation, devotion, and stretching. Done five times a day for a lifetime, it has profound effects on the body and soul.

Often, when people talk about bodyworks, they mean exercising the musculature and perhaps the inner organs. We should not forget that the body is also the breath, the circulatory system, the nervous system, and the endocrine system, as well as subtle electrical systems that rule the whole organism and are still poorly understood by science.

How we reflect the one cosmic energy will depend on the condition of this physical organism, and so it is necessary to consider the relaxation and the toning of the muscles, the purification of the inner organs, the awareness and rhythm of the breath; the detoxification and resonance of the nervous system; and the balanced and appropriate functioning of the endocrine system.

Whole books have been written on this subject and many extraordinary systems of body therapy exist. It is such a vast area that it is easy for one to get lost in. Although an intervention on any level will be reflected on other levels, healing on the highest levels of Spirit is most effective. Some simple guidelines can be instructive, and many illnesses and dangers can be avoided and the whole organism can be naturally harmonized when the soul is awake and loving.

We exist and have evolved in an electromagnetic sea. Our planet has a characteristic electromagnetic field strength and frequency. So does our nervous system, and it should not be a surprise that the two are closely related. The earth's magnetic field pulsates most strongly at a speed of eight to ten hertz. This corresponds with the alpha brain-wave frequency, the state of consciousness in which we feel most present. When our brain waves are pulsating faster than about ten hertz, we are in a state of superficial, reactive thought; we feel "speedy." This second state, beta, is the condition of modern society most of the time.

A third state, theta, is slower than the alpha frequency. Theta, five to six hertz, is most common in the state of sleep, although it is sometimes experienced by people when they are involved in creative expression or accessing the unconscious. If we could enter theta consciously, we would gain access to our own subconscious and to our own creative depths.

One of the ways in which our brain waves can be regulated is through conscious breathing. The alpha state is facilitated by a naturally deep and balanced breath, with equal inhalation and exhalation. The beta state is the product of irregular and shallow breathing. The usually unconscious theta state can be facilitated by increasing the length of time of exhalation, as in many forms of chanting or singing. The science of breathing is complex, and altering the breath can be hazardous. Still, we need to know enough to be as we are naturally meant to be, to overcome the abnormal conditions that are so common in our environments. For this a deep, balanced breath—with gratitude and awareness—will serve us well.

When we breathe consciously, we receive and digest the finer substances the air has to give. Being is nourished through the conscious assimilation of these substances. When we breathe unconsciously we receive what we need to keep alive, but when we breathe with awareness we nourish the life of the soul as well. It is impossible to overestimate the importance of conscious breathing.

An ever finer food is the food of impressions—all the sense perceptions processed by the nervous system. Here, too, consciousness is the elixir that transforms lead to gold, the unexamined life into eternal life, here and now. If we could awaken to the sounds, smells, sights, and sensations of our environment and purely receive these impressions with sensitive awareness, we would experience more life, and we would activate our nervous system more completely. So much of our nervous system has remained dormant because we are asleep to life. We experience life not as it is but through the medium of associations, preconceptions, and expectations.

Our nervous system has capacities for a much subtler and more perceptive relationship to life, but we have let ourselves be numbed. Any one of the senses has the capacity to awaken these subtle faculties. Frankincense in the liturgy of the Eastern Orthodox Church awakens the heart. The bell that is struck and fades at the beginning of Zen meditation stimulates the center between the eyebrows. The drumbeats of the shaman contain a bundle of frequencies that rhythmically stimulate the nervous system. The subtle intonations and change of pitch of Qur'anic recitation awaken many levels at once. The blue of the sky and the green of the leaves have specific capacities for spiritualizing and healing the nervous system—if we are conscious.

And just as the impressions of nature and sacred rituals can nourish the soul, other kinds of impressions can be like eating spoiled food. When we are in a negative state, we select the negative impressions from our environment. If we feed ourselves too much on negative impressions, we will experience negative results. The images presented to us in the media are so often of violence, ugliness, greed, and general disharmony, and these cannot contribute to a healthy and harmonious inner life—especially if we receive them unconsciously. With consciousness, however, we can both begin to discriminate what we take in and, if we are positive enough, transform negative impressions.

"Fasting is the bread of the Prophets, the sweet morsel of the saints," a teacher of mine would say. Fasting is meditation of the body, and meditation is fasting of the mind. Fasting helps the body to purify itself of the toxins that accumulate through the impurities of food and incomplete digestion.

Fasting, as long as it is not excessive, is based on a positive relationship to the body, for it eases the burdens the body must carry. Indulgence—whether in food, intoxicants, or pleasures—is a form of cruelty toward the body because of the price the body must pay for our so-called pleasures.

Purification leaves the body, especially the nervous system, in a more responsive state. Hunger reduces the need for sleep and increases wakefulness. Eating our fill hardens the heart, while hunger opens the heart and increases detachment. In hunger some of the veils between us and what is real are removed; remembrance becomes a way of life. Fasting has been a catalyst for awakening in all sacred traditions. Coleman Banks in *Open Secret* translates a Rumi saying this way: "If the brain and belly are burning clean with fasting, every moment a new song comes out of the fire."

With gratitude for being embodied, we will listen to what the body has to tell us. As always, gratitude will restore the proper perspective and remind us that the body is a means for awakening the soul.

Faithfulness
and Gracefulness

The inner search is from You.
The blind are cured by Your gift.
Without our searching, You gave us this search.
RUMI, *MATHNAWI*, I, 1337–38

 One of the most uncompromising women in history
was Rabia al-Adawiya. She is an extreme example of
faith, a woman who kept nothing in the mirror of her
heart but the Truth.

Malik-i Dinar tells the story of going to visit Rabia and finding her living with these few possessions: a broken pitcher from
which she drank and washed herself, an old straw mat, and a
brick she occasionally used as a pillow.

"I have friends with money," he told her. "If you want, I'll
get some for you."

"Malik, you're making a big mistake. Isn't my Provider and
theirs one and the same?"

"Yes," he replied.

"And has this Provider ever forgotten the poor because of
their poverty?"

"No," he said.

"And does It remember the rich, because of their riches?"

"No," he said.

"Then," she continued, "since He knows my state, why should I remind Him? If this is what He wants, this is what I want."

Rabia had such love for the Friend that she considered it almost a betrayal to want something other than what He wanted.

Once she was seriously ill when Hasan of Basra visited her. He met another man at the door who was weeping. The man told him, "I brought some medicine for Rabia and she will not accept it. If she dies it will be such a loss for humanity." So Hasan entered in the hope of convincing Rabia to be reasonable and accept the medicine. As soon as he walked in she spoke to him:

"If He provides for those who insult Him, won't He provide for those who love Him? Tell the man waiting outside not to cloud my heart with his offers. My Lord knows well what I need, and I only want what He wants for me."

One of the most important ideas is that of faith. In both the Gospels and in the Qur'an we are called to a state of faithfulness. Unfortunately, both the Arabic word *Iman* and the Greek word *pistis* have too often been translated as "belief." It has too often been said that it takes faith to believe in God, that the facts that we have cannot add up to a certainty of God, and that to believe in God is an act of faith. In other words, belief in God, or spirit, is not justified by the facts alone.

Most religions require belief in certain articles of faith and a verbal profession of faith. Catholics, for instance, must believe that Jesus is both a human being like us and also fully God. Muslims are asked to believe in the Day of Resurrection, in angels, and that the Qur'an is literally the word of God. In these cases—in what might better be called "conventional faith"—faith can mean the profession of a belief.

Faith, however, can be understood as hope substantiated by

knowledge. This is consistent with the Arabic etymological association of faith (*iman*) with verification. Faith is understood to
have an aspect of knowledge—a knowledge confirmed by the
heart. The principle of faith is the knowledge of the Unseen, Beneficent Being, a knowledge through the heart, or subtle faculties, because the spiritual reality is obvious neither to the senses
nor to the intellect.

The effect that derives from the root or principle of faith is
suggested by the word *faithful*. It does not necessarily suggest belief in any doctrine. To be faithful is to have a single reference
point. The lover will be faithful to the beloved; the mother will be
faithful to her family; the real warrior will be faithful to his cause.
Jesus rebuked his disciples for not having faith. Even the disciples
of Jesus could be said to be without real faith, and the word used
to describe them was *perverse*, a word that suggests a turning in
different directions in confusion.

To have faith means to have a center, an axis, a single point of
reference. And yet this point of reference is not necessarily apparent from the start; it is not automatically possessed. On the
contrary, the development of this faith will face many hazards
and doubts, because we are pulled in so many directions and are
so easily distracted.

For something to become a center for us it must in some way
be magnetic. The strongest, most magnetic reference point is
within us. This connection to the ground of Being is essentially
good and beautiful. We find and explore it by focusing our awareness on our essential Self through the heart.

Humanity suffers from its own incompleteness. We suffer
from being fragments and being fragmented to the extent that we
feel lonely, dependent, afraid, in conflict with ourselves, and subject to desires that must be controlled. We are grasping, clutch-
ing, and yearning most of the time.

The original meaning of *healing* was "to make whole." We can be healed of our separateness through our contact with something whole. We can know we are not separate from the whole, and we can know the universe through knowing ourselves. This is a statement of faith, or hope substantiated by knowledge.

Traditionally, faith has been the step following repentance. If we repent for our incompleteness, for the unending desires of the ego, and recognize our need of wholeness, that is the beginning of faith. Not until we sufficiently recognize our need can we be faithful and obedient to our own highest possibility. Once we have this kind of faith, even if we possess as little as a mustard seed of it, we can begin to practice with constancy—whether we are cleaning windows or polishing the mirror of the heart.

Already we have come rather far from the notion of faith as belief in doctrine. We can take a step farther and say that faith is a truly creative function. Isn't it said that with faith all things are possible? And that if two people join together in faith, the effect will be more than double? How is it that faith is creative?

Suppose that each of us has a certain quantity of psychic energy available to us during our lifetime, or during a single day for that matter. This quantity of psychic energy is being spent continually in all the trivial interests, petty anxieties and titillations, excitements, and disappointments that life brings. If we could bring our own being into a greater state of order and harmony, so that we could participate fully in what the moment brings and yet not suffer needless anxieties and distractions, and if we were to order our lives around a single value of magnetic power, the power of higher Being, it would not be surprising if we were to possess an unusual power of thought and feeling. If we make all our cares into a single care—the care for being tangibly in contact with the source of Life—that Life, that Creative Power, will attend to all those cares.

GRACE

Simone Weil said: "We must not wish for the disappearance of our troubles but the grace to transform them." Often when we wish our troubles would disappear, we are ignoring what could change in ourselves. We are confused between changing the outer circumstances, which may not be to our liking, and the way that we relate to them. Identified with circumstances and conditions, we may fall into resentment and think we must change the facts, when what we need to change is ourselves.

If we could see the arising of all events as opportunities to know and develop the qualities in ourselves, would we live in resentment toward what arises in each moment? With a center of gravity in Essence, a "yes" arises—the yes of recognition, rather than the no of resentment. Difficulty is first recognized, even before it is transformed. Trouble becomes a reminder that we can tap the infinite qualities of the Creative Power.

Through learning to participate in a certain dialog with this Power—an inner conversation that is both specific and spontaneous—we call upon the qualities we need to live fully, and we activate these qualities in ourselves: solidarity, courage, forgiveness, patience, or whatever is required. Every problem calls forth qualities from the treasury within us. Accepting more responsibility and challenges brings a greater activation.

How often we think that if only we didn't have these problems we would be free to relax and enjoy life! Meanwhile we are filled with the ordinary psychological toxins: self-pity, resentment, anger, fear, guilt, envy, and jealousy. We must convince the intellectual mind of the stupidity and futility of these things and put in their place the positive attributes of humbleness, gratitude, love, courage, emancipation, generosity, trust, and faith. We must do this in the workshop of the intellectual mind until it is quite clearly convinced, when the work will be shifted to the subconscious, superconscious mind. This is transformation.

Grace is always there. It is the life that flows from the Unknown Energizer of the universe. What we need to learn is to receive it and to become aware that grace is flowing from Life all the time. This Life is within us. All the qualities we might need are available if we can form the right connection. The three unlocking keys are humbleness, gratitude, and love. With these qualities we become receptive to grace.

We live in a time when there seem to be very few heroes. The original meaning of *hero* was someone favored by the gods and having godlike qualities. A hero is not without humbleness, which can be understood as our awareness of our dependence on Spirit. Gandhi was an example of both humbleness and heroism. Often humbleness exists because of the hero's connection to a higher aim: humbleness in front of a great Idea, in front of the infinity of Life. It is this kind of humility that leads to the forming of a connection with the infinite creative energy.

Faith becomes the absorption of all human faculties and attributes in the love of the One, or, if you will, the quest for Truth. As presence develops in us, so does faithfulness. Everything becomes harmonized by that presence. Finally that presence is unified in the One.

For most of us the work consists in asking within ourselves how we can meet the conditions of life positively, how we can improve the conditions around us, and how we can with faithfulness and gracefulness serve the needs we recognize.

The Alchemy of Effort

The porter runs to the heavy load and takes it from
    others,
knowing burdens are the foundation of ease
and bitter things the forerunners of pleasure.
See the porters struggle over the load!
It's the way of those who see the truth of things.
                    RUMI, *MATHNAWI*, II, 1834–36

*In my early twenties I lived in a spiritual community for the
first time. I lived with twenty or more residents in buildings of
mud brick high in the mountains, with a vast view of the desert
below. One morning when we were free of our usual work load, which
began at dawn, I had just begun to enjoy reading a book when my friend
John appeared. He had borrowed a flatbed truck and wanted to gather
some large rocks for a stone walk that was to be built. I was relishing the
leisure time I had in front of me and was in no mood to go off to dig and
lift large rocks. But John needed me, and he belittled all my excuses to the
point where I had no choice but to join him.*

*I was not in a very positive state about these developments. Neverthe-
less, I went along and found myself digging—not stones, but major boulders. John's idea was that most of the stone had to be buried in the ground
with only a small flat end showing on the surface. Each time I thought that
we had done the impossible and moved our last boulder, John would find*

another. It took several hours to find and load the necessary boulders. Then we returned to the community, the boulders secure on the flatbed as we slowly drove along the mountain roads. Standing on the flatbed just behind the cab with the wind blowing in my face, I felt some invisible shell crack, and I cried.

Effort is one of the methods by which we can spiritualize the mind, or in other words, create presence. When we consider the subject of effort, we must consider the forces of affirmation and denial that exist within each human being. Whenever we affirm something within ourselves through a real decision, we will inevitably bring into play a denying force, both within and without. If we affirm the wish to concentrate, we will encounter some distraction. If we affirm the wish to be active, we will encounter our passivity. If we decide to give, we will encounter that which withholds, and so forth.

We have within us a "yes" and a "no," and this is the basis of all effort. Something in us affirms while something else denies. We usually deal with our environment through personality, which consists of conditioning, acquired habits, and likes and dislikes. But we also have an essential Self, with essence qualities such as awareness, will, and love. This essential Self is usually buried beneath our awareness and our personality. Personality has taken the authority and the initiative; we act on the basis of what it desires and what it affirms. If we can submit to the higher Self, however, Essence can more and more become the affirming force in our lives, and the personality itself can be cultivated and brought into service.

Effort is not to be understood as the clash of opposites, but as the creation of a conscious presence, an "I Am." This presence includes the awareness of the "yes and no" within us. It stands above the clash of all opposites, balancing them.

Without the existence of denial there can be no work. It allows us to generate the energies essential to work by giving us the reason, the friction, and the fire to affirm our presence on a higher level. The mechanism of like and dislike will always remain, but through our conscious relationship to it we awaken Being in ourselves.

BEING AND IMPULSE

Our work is to awaken and realize a spiritual will and presence, a Being that is not coerced by like and dislike, the demands of the personality.

This spiritual will is enfeebled to the extent that we identify with every passing impulse. Many inner enemies must be faced, brought into submission, and finally transformed. Then, like the Prophet Muhammad, we may be able to say: "My Satan has become a faithful servant."

In a real human being two forces are at work: on one level, the potential for presence; on another, impulse, desire, and like and dislike. Both levels are necessary; both contribute to the working of the laws of transformation.

On the one hand all the impulses of the ego, arising from the history of our interaction with the world, represent a necessary force in life. The power of selfhood is not an essentially evil power, but it can go to excess when it divorces itself from the unity of life. In this condition of separation, the self becomes chaotic and antagonistic to life.

Our essential will and presence stands outside of time and space, relatively free and pure. This presence is more ourselves than the impulses with which we might identify. Some people may argue that to go with every impulse is natural and spontaneous; on the contrary, this response represents the depths of conditioning and mechanicality. It is not free will, but slavery. Freedom lies in the altogether different direction of conscious will that frees us from separation and opens us to unity.

The secret of transformation is the moment-by-moment alchemy of impulse. This may manifest itself as restraint in action and speech, as courtesy, self-discipline, generosity, subtlety, or patience. It is as if some thorny brambles appeared in our garden that we cut down to make room for the fruits and vegetables that will nourish us. Eventually there is the possibility, too, of a rose garden that represents pure beauty and spiritual fragrance, requiring the most conscious care. The power behind the ego is like that. It is not to be killed; it should be allowed to return in ever new and spiritualized forms.

That is why we must not give in easily to discouragement, complaint, or self-pity. Very often these attitudes are a sign that we have succumbed to what is trivial. We must practice the right kind of economy, using our substance and attention according to our highest values and aims. Then what was cut down will blossom. The ego we have denied expression will offer to serve. Enemies will return as friends, and the energy of discouragement will reappear as courage.

Effort begins with a decision and is sustained by the awareness of a "yes and no" within us. Through this healthy sense of effort we can begin to reflect true will and true human qualities, bringing greater joy into our lives. Through effort we can establish our connection with Spirit.

Effort releases energy for work. It is usually the body that carries the denying force in the form of desire. If we were to allow desire to dominate, if we were to follow every desire, we would end up dispersed, weakened, and dissolute. We can, however, counter the incessant desires of the body with some intention to work, to affirm something higher. The suppression of negativity does not help, because it never opens us to the transforming power of the finer energies. We are seeking the alchemical transformation of negativity through these finer energies.

Our real Self, our hidden treasure, is beyond our awareness and our personality, but we can find a channel to it. This channel is created through the presence of finer energies in us, and these energies are the result of a certain work. Their presence in our nervous system helps us to connect to subtler states of Being.

Aim and Self-Knowledge

The mouse soul is nothing but a nibbler.
To the mouse is given a mind proportionate to its
    need,
for without need, the Almighty God
doesn't give anything to anyone.
Need, then, is the net for all things that exist:
man has tools in proportion to his need.
So, quickly, increase your need, needy one,
that the sea of abundance may surge up in loving-
    kindness.

RUMI, *MATHNAWI*, II, 3279–80; 3292

People become obsessed with their ego-driven goals,
forgetting that the present moment is the source of well-
being and fulfillment. Goal-oriented behavior has come
under critical analysis in recognition of this tendency for goals to
become more important than the quality of process through
which they are realized. To the extent that we are more interested
in having than in being, in imagining our ultimate gratification
than in giving consent to this moment, we fall into obsessive
goal-oriented activity.

At the other extreme, som people use spirituality as a justification for their aimlessness and lack of discipline. Living without

exercising conscious choice is failing to use that attribute which makes us most uniquely human. Without exercising our wills we are living at the level of animal life. If an animal is given access to a drug that brings it pleasure, such as cocaine, it will self-administer the drug to the point of death. Human beings have reason and conscious will to enable them to step outside their instinctual drives and unconscious behavior. We are equipped to take responsibility for self-actualization.

There is much to be learned from archery. In the Zen tradition, archery is sometimes the occasion for training and realization. The archer learns to hit the target without trying. Muhammad, as well, recommended archery as one of the most beneficial pastimes. Through the coming together of archer, arrow, and target, three may become one; but without the target, archer and arrow become meaningless.

So too in the inner life. Without an aim, the necessary creative tension does not exist. We do not practice, and we waste the substance of our will and attention. And yet the aim is just one aspect of a whole, to be included within this present moment without obscuring it.

Having a definite aim is a reminder, not a limitation. If it is an aim that has developed out of a spiritual yearning, rather than from some demand of the ego, it has the possibility of connecting us with the whole of the Work. This kind of aim most often involves some activation of presence or awakening.

People may have some difficulty in formulating an aim in the beginning, and this is usually because they have not acquired enough self-knowledge. One of the first aims is to acquire more knowledge of ourselves—to know what kind of people we habitually are. Self-knowledge is gained by observing ourselves in light of the Work.

We can learn to observe more, to catch those fleeting moments of judgment, greed, fear, and resentment that poison us inside. We can learn to recognize the degree of our separateness in the form of envy, resentment, pride, or hypocrisy. We can begin to notice our lack of presence in the form of daydreaming and inner talking, unconscious lying, justifying, and gossiping. This is never a painless experience, but once we have committed ourselves to the search for truth, to seeing ourselves as we really are, we must see without judging what we see.

The work before us includes a new way of thinking. When our own ego was our center of gravity we could excuse and justify ourselves; we could find fault outside of ourselves and shift responsibility. With this new way of thinking and seeing we have less invested in the ego and thus less to protect. We also become more sensitive to the poisoning of our inner life that results from certain kinds of thoughts and feelings. Previously the ego, which never sees that it is asleep, could justify and excuse itself, but now it sometimes feels itself disarmed. We bring a new set of values face-to-face with our inner selves, and we see ourselves as if with new eyes. We desire to be more inwardly clean, to accept a life under different laws. Witnessing our envy, resentment, pride, and hypocrisy helps to lessen our own illusion of separation. Working with wrong talking, lying, and gossiping helps to preserve the force of the Work inside us. Transcending fear and judgment, and like and dislike, liberates us from the prison of our conditioning.

WORK WITH WEAKNESSES

As we become more grounded in self-knowledge, we are able to begin working with our weaknesses. Weakness leads to weakness, just as strength leads to strength. It is useful to focus on a particular weakness and begin to work with it. For instance, someone who has a tendency to overeat or has some compulsive habit such as smoking or gossiping can decide to work with this tendency. If we are habitually critical of others, we can try to bear with some of those things we dislike. If we are impatient, we can practice patience. If we often fail to complete cycles, we can determine to complete them. If we sometimes do not keep our word, we can decide to do more than we say. If we neglect to pay our share, we can become givers. If we are resentful or bitter, we can practice gratitude. If we are selfish and possessive, we can decide to give away things that are precious to us. If we are lazy, we can ask more of ourselves. If we tend to think of ourselves as very special, we can try to see how we are like everyone else. If we have too low an opinion of ourselves, we can learn to respect who we are.

Any attempt to work with a weakness must be approached intelligently and sensitively. Our choice of a weakness to address should be based on careful observation and self-knowledge. With this self-knowledge a real personal aim becomes possible; we have observed ourselves long enough to begin some specific work on the kind of people we habitually are. Aim can be too general, too difficult, or simply inappropriate. An aim should be specific and attainable, and it should be consistent with the general aim of the Work, which is awakening.

WORK ON AWAKENING

To work on awakening is to extract attention or awareness from the stream of events, to cultivate an awareness that includes events, thoughts, and feelings but is not totally absorbed, or identified with them. It involves an intention above all to be actively receptive, to be alive with sensitivity and attention, not to be thoroughly identified with one's conditioning. Our intention to be awake is helped by deciding to interrupt our unconsciousness by setting intentional alarms for ourselves. Some simple examples of this might be to awaken presence before the first bite of a meal, as we walk through any door, whenever a phone rings, or whenever we use the word *I*.

The development of will, working with clear intentions, completing cycles, keeping our promises, and being on time all contribute to awakening and remaining awake.

WORK ON BALANCE

Another category of aims has to do with becoming balanced people. With a balanced consciousness we can think without being dominated by our thinking; we can feel, but are not tyrannized by our feelings; and we can take care of our bodies without being slaves to them. Intellectuals, for instance, may need to work with their bodies or with developing feelings, whereas physical, instinctual types may need to develop the mind through study. Those living mostly from their emotions may need to curb their sentimentality, self-pity, or anger through right thinking.

DECISION

Once an aim is visualized and decided upon, it is to be faithfully carried out. Every decision that is put into action, no matter how small, will contribute to the development of conscious will and freedom. Conversely, every decision that we fail to act on will rob us of will. Making conscious decisions and completing cycles can with practice become a healthy way of life.

The exercise of the will through conscious decision is our birthright. If we fail to develop an integrated, viable selfhood and to use our wills in a healthy way, we will fail to come up to the level of true human beings. But the development of our humanity has its paradoxes: In one breath we speak of integrating the self and in the next, of transcending it.

Emancipation from Fear

Look at yourself, trembling,
afraid of non-existence:
know that non-existence is also afraid
that God might bring it into existence.
If you grasp at worldly dignities,
it's from fear, too.
Everything, except love of the Most Beautiful,
is really agony. It's agony
to move towards death and not drink the water
    of life.

RUMI, *MATHNAWI*, I, 3684–87

The spiritual journey from beginning to end can be characterized as the overcoming of fear. A whole philosophy and methodology could be developed around this fact. Fear shapes the false self and fuels its desires. Our preoccupation with fear is the greatest obstacle standing between us and the abundant life we might know.

As Rumi says, much of human life is really agony—disguised and unconscious, perhaps, but nevertheless a low-grade agony

prolonged by fears and unfulfilled desires. The human condition
is governed by fear. We are afraid of imaginary losses and difficulties that we may never encounter. A nameless undercurrent of
fear runs through many of our relationships. One man may fear
his neighbor's children; employers may fear the people they employ; workers may be afraid of their boss; and the boss may be
afraid of someone's lawyer, who in turn may be afraid of his son.

Surrounded with our material comforts and lulled by our
imagined independence, we are unlikely to realize the extent of
the fears that control us. Yet unconsciously we carry unreason-
able and imaginary fears that not only wear away at our happiness
but also prevent the inflow of Spirit. The more our sense of identity and well-being is determined by extrinsic factors, by things
that we possess or by what people think of us, the more we are unaware of our own intrinsic worth and the more we are enslaved
to the fear of loss.

The transformation of fear can serve as a model of how any
negative emotion may be changed. Presence can heal our subconscious resistance and awaken us to our essential well-being.
Presence is *seeing,* sustaining a conscious relationship to our experience. Yet most of the time we are identified with our experience. Our first need is to wish to awaken and be present.
Through conscious breathing, through being grounded in an
awareness of our bodiliness, through meditation, and through
conscious movement, we can cultivate the state of presence.

With presence we can begin to observe our inner life, open
up to our feelings, reflect on our motivations, and notice how we
act. We can keep in mind the question of how fear influences our
lives. If we keep this question before us, we will extend our
awareness and increase our understanding of how fear operates
in us.

Presence is the space around our inner and outer experiences. In a sense, we are that space. With it we can allow transfor-

mation to happen. We can allow fear to be seen and eventually to be dissolved by that seeing.

We may begin by noticing the small fears that control us. We have fears of being criticized and rejected, of being alone and separate—unconscious, nagging fears that drain us because we are not conscious of them. They have power because we deny their existence. Once recognized and examined, they lose much of their power over us.

If we have identified particular fears that are stubbornly persistent, we can begin to reason with the subconscious mind, to convince it that its fear is not productive. Our subconscious has been shaped by unconscious associations, by miseducation, and by random programming from our environment. Using the intellect, that part of the mind that we can consciously direct and control, we can reprogram the subconscious. We can corner it, talk with it, and reason with it.

One way to overcome those fears that have a paralyzing effect on us is to be decisive and challenging. Too often we childishly cover our eyes and ears, when what we need to do is squarely face our fears. We might, for instance, tell the subconscious: "You are afraid of not being loved and so you hide your real self. You play a role, afraid to show yourself as you are. But meanwhile you suffer this abandonment in your imagination a thousand times. Wouldn't it be better to be abandoned once rather than a thousand times? And wouldn't it be better not to have to pretend? Isn't your real self more lovable than your role-playing self? How did you ever talk yourself into living this lie? Why not face the possibility of loss, once and for all? What is there to lose?"

This process of conscious reasoning is different from our ordinary inner talking. When we reason with ourselves consciously, we are motivated by our highest understanding. In the spaciousness of presence we are using the faculty of will, of conscious choice, by reframing the situation to induce transformation. The subconscious somehow became convinced that fear was necessary; we can convince it otherwise. We have a right to be free of unnecessary fear.

We also struggle with what could be considered justifiable fears. We have fears of loss, pain, disability, and death. These fears can be transformed only by the human being who has come to know what it means to "die before you die." In the discipline of transformation, this expression means coming to know our spiritual home, our eternal Self. It is not a metaphor but an accurate description of a psychospiritual truth.

Many of those who have lived through the experience of a clinical death and have returned to life know that death is not something to fear and that life is an immeasurable gift. These people return to their lives with less fear because they have experienced their metaphysical home. At the same time they have known that this physical body is important as a means of contact with their fellow human beings. Against the backdrop of eternity this transient human life has acquired a new beauty.

To die before death is to detach from our physical body, thoughts, and emotions at will. This is the aim of certain forms of spiritual training. Through control of the breath, fasting, and sustained awareness it becomes possible to separate from our coarser bodies and to mount the steed of pure consciousness. When consciousness is separated from the conditioned intellect and desire, it makes a direct contact with the electromagnetic field of Love. The soul comes to know a different relationship to all the beings within this electromagnetic field. When we are connected with this Love, we are free from fear and from the domination of the rational mind. As Rumi said, "Reason is powerless in the expression of love." Love is reckless and does not count the cost; Love engenders courage and self-sacrifice. Often our fear is a lack of love. To be free of fear we must love very much.

According to 'Attar's *Remembrance of the Saints,* a group of prominent Sufis were denounced as blasphemous heretics before the Caliph of Baghdad. The Caliph ordered them to appear before him. Without trial the Caliph ordered these five pious men—Abu Hamza, Raqqam, Shebli, Nuri, and Junaid—to be immediately slain. The executioner was about to slay Raqqam when Nuri thrust himself fearlessly into Raqqam's place. Laughing with joy, he cried, "Kill me first!"

"It's not your turn yet," the executioner said, "and a sword should not be wielded too hastily."

"I wish to die first. I prefer my friends to myself. Life is the most precious thing in this world, and I would like to give the last minutes of my life to serving my brothers. I do this even though one moment in this world is dearer to me than a thousand years in the next. For this world is the place of service, while the other world is the place of intimacy with God. But intimacy for me is here in service."

These words of Nuri were reported to the Caliph, who eventually freed all the men, saying, "If these men are unbelievers, then I declare that on the face of this earth, not one true believer exists."

The Caliph summoned the men before him and asked, "Is there anything you want from me?"

"Yes," they replied. "Forget us. We want neither your honor nor your banishment. The two are the same to us."

The Caliph wept bitterly and dismissed them all with honor.

The state of emancipation toward which we are journeying is freedom from the fear of loss. It is understood that life flows to us from an unstinting Source of grace that will never lessen its giving as long as we are open to receiving. The people and things that are so precious to us are embodiments of qualities, and these qualities derive from this beneficent Source. What we are so afraid of losing are qualities that we have discovered and invested in the particular forms we are attached to. We have confused these qualities with the *forms* we have discovered them in. Their beauty is like the beauty of sunlight that falls upon a brick wall:

Sunlight fell upon the wall;
the wall received a borrowed splendor.
Why set your heart on a piece of earth, simple one?
Seek out the source which shines forever.
RUMI, *MATHNAWI*, II, 708–709

The wall may crumble or be torn down, but the sun will always return to shine. To be spiritually mature is to be free of the fear of loss, knowing we are connected to the Source of all generosity.

Jesus said so many times, "Fear not." And as one of my teachers said, "A seeker would never offer fear as an excuse for anything. Fear is not accepted by one who has a quest." So what are we to make of the fear of God?

Unfortunately, certain translators have used the word *fear* in relation to God. But is God to be literally feared? In the Qur'an the word *takwa* is often translated as "fear," but is would be better translated as "vigilance," "awe," or "God-consciousness." It is the awareness of being in the presence of the Beloved; it is an impeccable alertness that keeps us aware of the consequences of our actions. In the presence of the Beloved, one's attention should be absorbed in the Beloved. A lover who was always fretting distractedly in the presence of his or her beloved would not be a lover at all. The lover has only one fear, and that is the fear of offending the Beloved (which includes harming other people). The fear of God frees the lover of all other fears. Perhaps that fear, that caution, that circumspection is a desirable quality in one who is courting the Truth.

Suffering:
Imaginary and Real

If you wish your misery to end,
seek also to lose your wisdom—
the wisdom born of human illusion,
that which lacks the light
of God's overflowing grace.
The wisdom of this world increases doubt;
the wisdom of faith releases you into the sky.

RUMI, *MATHNAWI*, II, 3200–203

Two kinds of suffering can be recognized in this world, one imaginary and one real. Dissolving the imaginary suffering prepares us to bear the real suffering. Imaginary suffering comes from our illusions about life and about ourselves. If we are dominated by the false self, we will suffer with all the denial and misplaced resistance it offers to reality. This imaginary suffering, which is sometimes trivial and other times intense, is a suffering, that we have created for ourselves.

Real suffering has to do with the world we live in. Some of this is from natural causes, such as illness, accident, disaster, and death, and much of it, including poverty, hunger, pollution, hatred, cruelty, violence, and tyranny, is the result of unconscious human actions. As long as human beings are unconscious and dominated by selfish and illusory desires, there is no god who will force us to change. But as the history of revelation on earth testifies, guidance has come to all communities and nations from wise persons and sacred books. Humanity has been reminded and warned. That is as much as Cosmic Intelligence can do; the burden of responsibility rests on each individual human heart.

The faithful, the believers, are those who recognize through reason and through the heart that an Unseen Beneficence exists. The unbelievers are those who follow only the god of their egos, whose wills create disharmony and go beyond all bounds. Dominated by their illusions, such people are fated to suffer being out of harmony, at the same time that they contribute to the objective suffering of the world.

Unbelievers see this world as nothing but illusion. Yet our existential reality can neither be reduced to mere illusion nor to a concatenation of absurd and meaningless facts. At the same time, Sufism does not view this life as either the comfortless zone of temptation and testing or as that sentimental version of reality in which everything works out for the best.

The Sufis have embraced a unified reality comprised of worlds of greater and lesser subtlety coexisting. This reality has attributes that can be classified into two main categories: on the one hand, qualities of beneficence, mercy, intimacy, and beauty; and on the other, qualities of majesty, power, and wrath. The former qualities have precedence over the latter. In this truly holistic view of reality, both tenderness and destructiveness have their place. One of the sayings of Muhammad known as a *hadith qudsi,* in which he transmitted knowledge of the Divine, is "Take refuge in My Mercy from My Wrath. Take refuge in Me from Me." In other words, God is not only the suffering of the world, but the refuge within this suffering as well.

The suffering of the world adds to the reality of Spirit. Reality teaches us by means of opposites and contrasts. Eventually we understand and appreciate the necessity of this balance between these two categories of mercy and wrath. The precedence of mercy, however, is shown when we learn that even the wrath is a disguised form of mercy. As Rumi says:

> *Pain is a treasure of Mercy;*
> *the fruit is juicy when you peel the rind.*
> MATHNAWI, II, 2261

> *The unsuspecting child first wipes the tablet*
> *and then writes the letters on it.*
> *God turns the heart into blood and desperate tears;*
> *then writes the spiritual mysteries on it.*
> MATHNAWI, II, 1826–27

If the suffering and drama of this world were not real, unconditional Love would have no place. The imperfection of the world is what gives birth to the reality of Love—an unconditional Love that loves even this imperfection. Love is a quality of the unconditioned and infinite that penetrates this imperfect and conditioned world, bringing with it a taste of beauty and mercy. If Love were reserved only for the lovable it would not be cosmic. The mystery and mercy of Love is that we are its recipients despite our faults and weaknesses. Knowing this is what allows us to love even our enemies and to love more of this imperfect world.

One of the most common practices among Sufis is to begin their activities by inwardly reciting the phrase "In the name of God, the Most Compassionate and Merciful." From the nondualistic perspective of esoteric spirituality this means "Let me be and manifest Compassion and Mercy, since there is no other agent than the infinitely Compassionate One."

That life in the world is full of suffering is undeniable, but spirituality is not our insulation from this suffering. Presence allows us to open to the suffering of the world; compassion is being able to feel the world's suffering without being drowned by it. Perhaps it is in accepting our servanthood, in opening to the suffering of the world, that we ourselves are further transformed and acquire the qualities of the Creative Power.

Lovingkindness is drawn to the saint,
as medicine goes to the pain it must cure.
Where there is pain, the remedy follows:
wherever the lowlands are, the water goes.
If you want the water of mercy, make yourself low;
then drink the wine of mercy and be drunk.
Mercy upon mercy rises to your head like a flood.
RUMI, *MATHNAWI*, II, 1938–40

Die Before You Die

How much the Beloved made me suffer
before this work settled into the eye's water
and the liver's blood.
A thousand fires and smokes and its name is Love!
A thousand pains and regrets and afflictions—
and its name is Beloved!
Let every enemy of his own false self set to work!
Welcome to the self's sacrifice and pitiful death!

RUMI, *DIVAN*, 12063

 A Sufi came to a remote village where he knew no one. After meeting some people he found that those of this village had an unusual hunger for spiritual knowledge. They invited him to share his knowledge at a gathering they would arrange. Although this Sufi was not yet fully confident that he could transmit spiritual knowledge, he accepted their invitation. Many people attended that gathering and the Sufi found his audience to be extremely receptive to what he had to say, and most significantly, he found that he was able to express the teachings he had received with an eloquence he had never before experienced. He went to sleep that night feeling very pleased.

The next day he met one of the elders of the village. They greeted each other as brothers, and the elder expressed his gratitude for the previous evening. The Sufi was beginning to feel very special. He even reasoned to

himself that he had been guided to this village to impart the wisdom that he had accumulated through his long years of training and service. Perhaps, if these people were sincere, he could stay with them for awhile and really offer them some extended instruction in the Way of Love and Remembrance. They were certainly a deserving and sincere community. Just then, the elder invited him to another gathering that evening.

The villagers assembled again that evening, but this time one of them was chosen at random to address the gathering. He, too, gave a most eloquent discourse, full of wisdom and love. After the meeting the Sufi again met with the elder. "As you can see," the elder began, "the Friend speaks to us in many forms. We are all special here and we are all receptive to the Truth and so the Truth can easily express Itself. Know that the 'you' who felt special last night and the 'you' who felt diminished tonight are neither real. Prostrate them before the inner Friend if you want to find wisdom and be free of judging yourself harshly."

There is an underlying attitude that cripples and blinds us. It can be so pervasive that we don't often question it. This attitude is a perversion of the natural order created by our loneliness and insecurity, by the illusion of separateness, by ignorance. The problem, in a way, is quite simple: we think of ourselves too often and in the wrong way. The result is self-importance (or its opposite, self-hatred) and greed.

Whenever we think we are better than others or whenever we think "I want," we are thinking of ourselves in the wrong way. When we can think differently—"my family needs this, my body needs this, my work needs this, help me to meet these needs, help me to reflect Your abundance"—we can open to the inflow of spiritual energy.

Self-importance and greed take us out of presence and into identification. It makes no difference whether we are greedy about things that are harmful to us or for so-called spiritual experiences—neither is helpful. Self-importance and greed can spoil our efforts toward knowledge and presence.

We can begin to notice when we are thinking of ourselves too much and can turn from getting to giving. If we stop thinking about ourselves in a mechanical or compulsive way, we can better be what we are. True service is giving of ourselves, of what we naturally are. Becoming a human being is learning how to give, even more than learning how to meditate or exercise the will. Meditation and exercising the will are not the goal; we practice them to decondition ourselves and undermine our self-importance and greediness.

Because of our self-centered, egotistical point of view we cannot see things as they are. Because we are identified with our lower self, we suffer through whatever difficulties we meet. But these difficulties and sufferings are all a kind of mercy in disguise. Through this suffering we may learn to abandon our attachment to ourselves and attain knowledge of the Self.

Through taking a look at our pain, we may come to realize that we are always in suffering because of our attachment to ourselves and our separation from or ignorance of the One. Our pain is the Friend's invitation to His presence; suffering is the threshold of the One. As Rumi says, "Whoever is more awake has more pain. Seek pain!"

And so we need not resent suffering; we can accept it with the knowledge that it makes us more aware of our identification with the false self and our separation from Truth. The more we consciously bear suffering and pain, the more we will enter the presence of the One. When we are suffering we can remember to take refuge in the One. Having decided to enter the fire of love, we learn to take whatever is given to us without complaint.

There was once a king who gave generously to those in need. On one day he would give to widows, on another to the lame, on a third to the blind, and on a fourth to poor students. His only requirement was that those in need should wait in silence. There was one poor student, however, who could not keep from whining when the king approached. The student was, of course, ignored. On the next day he dressed himself in rags and stood with those suffering from illness, but the king recognized him. On another day he dressed up like an old widow, but still the king somehow recognized him. This went on day after day, and always the king recognized the impostor. Finally, however, he wrapped himself in a death shroud and lay down on the side of the road. The king, when he passed by, dropped some gold pieces to pay for the burial. Then the student's hand and head appeared from within the shroud to claim the gold pieces before someone else picked them up. Seeing that the king was watching, he said, "Do you see how at last I have received something from your generosity?"

"Yes," said the king, "But not before you died!"

Rumi says:

> *The mystery of "Die before you die" is this:*
> *that the gifts come after your dying, and not before.*
> *Except for dying, you artful schemer,*
> *no other skill impresses God. One Divine gift*
> *is better than a hundred kinds of exertion.*
> *Your efforts are assailed from a hundred sides,*
> *and the favor depends on your dying.*
> *The trustworthy have already put this to the test.*
> MATHNAWI, VI, 3837–40

We could complain of the Beloved, asking, "Why do you inflict such pain on someone you love? Do you want to shed the blood of the innocent?"

The Beloved would answer, "Yes, My Love kills only the innocent."

Within each human being is a vast Creative Power, a hidden treasure, but this treasure is not something we can possess. It is sweet, but it is not something that we can eat. By appropriating its qualities to ourselves, we short-circuit the system. When we claim no qualities as our own, we will have the qualities of this Creative Power. It is said that the Friend never takes away your self without giving you Himself. I will not worry about my life being separate from all life; my life will be seen in everything.

Rumi says, "Only he who is an enemy to his own existence possesses real existence." This is not advice for the immature. Not until we can forgo the impulses of the small, compulsive self will we be able to tap the infinite dimension of mind. *Without dying, the soul cannot come to life.*

What you thought was your self was an isolated fragment of your mind, containing contradictory desires, conditionings, and obsessions. With awareness and love this false self can dissolve like ice in sunlight.

Submission is the lower self recognizing the essential Self and acting on its guidance. It is overcoming the resistance offered by the lower self. It is to drop the hesitations, doubts, fears, equivocations, rationalizations, resentments, and suspicions that keep us from expressing the great Self.

At a higher stage, once union has been glimpsed, the mere separation from the Beloved becomes an even greater suffering than our ordinary psychological sufferings. Only then can you unify your conscious awareness with your essential Self and access your finest intuition. The impulses arising in you will be authentic and appropriate—those of a true human being.

When we can listen to and express that Self, we will find what is needed to meet life's demands. Having brought the conscious mind into resonance with a dimensionless point within, which contains all qualities in potential, each of us comes spontaneously to the Truth. We will be able to embrace life and those we need to love. This dimensionless point within is our point of contact with the qualities of Spirit. If we can regularly silence the mind and be aware at this core of our being, we will receive help from the Source of life. Presence is the empty center that attracts and manifests the qualities of Spirit.

The Freedom
of the Soul

Two stones cannot occupy the same space,
but two fragrances can.

The freedom of the soul depends on our becoming
aware of our existence as the intersection of many
worlds. Higher worlds have fewer laws and therefore
greater freedom. It is our destiny to be free—free in our souls, not
in our egos. If our souls were free, we would not suffer from the
limitations of this earthly existence.

/ Spiritual freedom depends on being conscious as a soul. In
the body we may know restriction. We may be limited in physical
capabilities, such as when we are ill or weak. We may be restricted by not being able to be in Katmandu because we must be
in Boston. At best we might be able to acquire enough financial
independence to allow us to move around more freely, but perhaps that independence will cost us time and effort. This is the
nature of the space-time prison we live in. The first freedom is
the realization that the material world can never satisfy us, although we are more or less enslaved to it. The material world,
which is under so many laws and restrictions, does little for our

Being. Even if we learn to manipulate this material world very well, it does not necessarily bring us closer to life itself. However much we can do in this world is not enough. We must have inner development, a contact with an inner knowing. Disillusionment with the material world does not mean that we turn our backs on it, but that we remember what it cannot of itself give us.

At higher levels, there are fewer laws. Two stones cannot occupy the same space, but two fragrances can. In the world of solid material existence, a stone has a weight and mass that limits what it can do. Fragrance, on the other hand, being matter in molecular form, has powers of diffusion and penetration that allow it to spread at phenomenal speeds over great distances in all directions at once. A rock, however, can move only if it is moved, and then only in a single direction and at a speed limited by the force acting on it.

The difference between matter in its solid state and matter in its molecular state is analogous to the mind limited by the ordinary intellect and senses and the mind that has become spiritualized. The latter has certain properties that would be considered miraculous: the ability to be in more than one place at a time, to interpenetrate matter, to pass through barriers, and to coexist in the same space with bodies of a similar material. Subtilization leads to freedom. The world of the senses is the most restricted world we live in.

In addition to living in the material world, the world of sense perception and physical being, we also live in a world of emotion and thought. At this level we are restricted, if a little less so. It is at the level of our thinking and feeling that we form a satisfactory relationship to the material world. We may be poor materially but rich in inner experience. This is the level where meaning and value are superimposed on the concrete facts of life. Negative thoughts and attitudes spoil everything; positive ones can affect and transform our perceptions.

Many people have emotional habits that restrict them. A

child abandoned by its mother at an early age may carry over something from that event. A person who has been shamed too many times may internalize that shame and acquire a negative self-image. Someone who has ceased to have new and adventurous experiences might crystallize into certain rigid patterns of emotional response. Unless we consciously break up certain patterns and maintain our flexibility, we may suffer emotional restriction. The person whose Essence is not enslaved by the personality will be less invested in the personality and therefore less protective of its own false image. Someone who has learned to become "nothing" will be able to manifest Spirit with a greater range of qualities.

At the level of thought we may also suffer restriction, a lack of freedom through concepts that are too limiting. Conventional social life fills us with such concepts as "a man never cries," "a lady would never do such a thing," "my country right or wrong," and so forth. On the path of transformation it is necessary to awaken from the sleep of the conventional social self, to put all of one's conditioning into question. It is necessary to see how one's concepts and opinions have shaped one's reality.

Compulsive and repetitive habits of thought or behavior lead one to become more fixed in one's personality and to fall further and further under the domination of the personality. By working to free ourselves from negative thought forms and negative emotions, we can become free to think creatively with greater focus and consciousness and to open our feelings to impressions of the present moment.

There is a kind of thought, which we call *delusion,* that leads us further from the real world and into greater slavery. If we are under too much delusion we will eventually be institutionalized. We could become so unaware of the consequences of our actions that we might jump out of a window, thinking we can fly, dreaming we are free. With this delusion we might end up injured or dead. A Sufi once said, "We can't break natural law but we can break our necks trying." Is it possible that most of mankind is suffering from a maleficent delusion that causes us to be blind to the consequences of our actions?

Most people are comfortable in their prisons, just like the parakeet who, when we open the door to his cage, often tries to close it with his beak. If a parakeet does this we may think it is amusing, but if people restrict themselves, we have to call their behavior stupid but typical. Nothing is accomplished by this action except the creation of a comforting delusion to support our own self-imposed restrictions.

Some kinds of thoughts can actually help us to remain open, flexible, and aware. Spiritual thoughts may serve as reminders, as doors into new perceptions. Early in my Sufi training I was told, "The seeker [dervish or Sufi] stands at the threshold between freedom and slavery." A Sufi is called the son or daughter of the moment, because he or she learns to live on the fine edge of conscience and awareness.

A greater freedom is available to us when we can free ourselves from the domination of demands from body, emotion, and thought. There is a level of consciousness in which these things do not have control. Greater consciousness implies greater choice, greater adaptability.

As we learn to make our home in consciousness or presence, we feel free within our circumstances—even without changing them. This may be the only true freedom. When we are conscious in this way, we also find a relaxed grounding in the body. It is good to have as much physical health and flexibility as possible, as it is to have maximal health and flexibility of emotions and thought. But no freedom can be compared to the freedom of the soul, a freedom without need, expectation, or worry.

The freedom of the soul frees one from our greatest slavery, the unlimited demands of the ego. The greatest freedom is in being free not to satisfy the ego's demands. Inner freedom is being able to choose one's attitude and to direct one's attention.

There is no such thing as absolute freedom. We are in bondage to the material world, to genetics, and to all the laws of nature; we may also be in bondage to money, sex, and power. Alternatively we may be in bondage to Spirit, the only true power. If I can become a servant of Spirit, I will be free of many laws; I will be answerable to only one thing, and there is a freedom in that. Ultimate servanthood is ultimate freedom. Muhammad said, "Make all your cares into a single care and God will see to all your cares."

The servanthood of the spiritual world is the servanthood to Love, which is no bondage at all, because it is itself so satisfying. Jesus and Muhammad in a sense were not free, because neither of them had any choice—both were submitted to Love.

If we find ourselves suffering from the ego, either in conflict with another or with ourselves, Love is the remedy. May we put ourselves in bondage to Love.

If we find ourselves suffering in anticipation, or from memories, let us practice freedom from the self and reliance on the One. The egocentric view is that everything happens in the universe because of ourselves. A young child whose parents divorce may believe that he or she is in some way responsible for the divorce. Some people are so sensitive that they take everything personally, and some are so spoiled and used to having things their own way that they take everything as a reflection of themselves too. In both cases, it is a sense of "I" that restricts. It is this sense that can undergo a positive change.

Being in relationship to the Creative Power cannot be compared to any other freedom. What is freedom, if not a spontaneous connection to this power? It is the freedom from the restriction of the ego, a lack of anticipation through living fully in the moment, the possibility of choosing an attitude and a relationship to circumstances, a generosity and willingness to take risks without fear of loss, and the activation of true resourcefulness in Love.

Most people are satisfied with their slavery, but some come together because they recognize another possibility. The Work informs us that freedom is found in surrender, trust, and friendship with the One. This freedom grows as we discover the qualities of the Friend within ourselves: generosity, patience, acceptance, truthfulness, and courage. We can become emancipated from the ego and come to know the invulnerability of the Essence we are. We were made to know the freedom of a timeless, eternal soul fully engaged in this Life.

What We Love
We Will Become

Whatever it is you wish to marry,
go absorb yourself in that beloved,
assume its shape and qualities.
If you wish for the light, prepare yourself
to receive it; if you wish to be far from God,
nourish your egoism and drive yourself away.
If you wish to find a way out of this ruined prison,
don't turn your head away from the Beloved,
but bow in worship and draw near.

RUMI, *MATHNAWI*, I, 3605–607

 Sitting beneath a tree in a park was a poor man quietly murmuring, "Oh God, God, God. . . ." Many people must have passed without notice or care, until someone sarcastically remarked: "I hear you calling God, but I don't hear God answering." The poor man was thrown into perplexity. Time passed and some tears flowed before a messenger from God appeared and said, "Brother, your Lord wants you to know that your calling Him IS His answer to you."

The soul is a ray of Spirit at the center of a human being. It is the soul's nature to be impressionable, to take on the qualities of whatever it identifies with, whatever it desires or loves. If it identifies with its social conditioning, it will take on those qualities. If it is identified with miscellanous desires, it will reflect their contradictions. If it identifies primarily with its instinct, it takes on animal qualities. If it identifies with Spirit, it takes on the qualities of Spirit.

Whatever the soul chooses to love, it will resemble. And therefore what we choose to love is important: Love is the force behind every level of existence. There is some good in every attraction, but there is a process of refining attraction, of choosing what to love, so that we are energized by a wider, purer love.

At first love operates as attraction or desire, as eros, choosing among the many forms that the material world offers. We strive for satisfaction in the emotional and psychological realms. We are identified with the forms we desire, especially through our likes and dislikes, our attractions and our aversions. This love is characterized by love of the desirable, the lovable, and by possessiveness.

Love at another level is sharing with others, or *philos*. There is a beauty in just being able to share a time and a place with others. Relationship broadens the self and tames the ego. Marriage, family, and community form widening spheres of abundant life. *Philos* is sharing and empathy.

But there is a love greater than attraction or sharing, and it is said to be the love for Spirit—objective love, or *agape*. Spirit within us can love Spirit in everything. In this love we are loving what we are. The duality between you and "the other" has dissolved, and what remains is a field of love.

Love is seeking itself. This cosmic electromagnetic milieu in which we exist offers possibilities of bonding, relationship, and communion. Our openness, our relatedness, and our engagement are the measure of our love. The more we purify ourselves of our self-centeredness, the more we will feel the benefits of this love.

What we find most beautiful, inspiring, and magnetic will draw us out. It is the degree of Spirit in anything that is its beauty. Sometimes we mistake glamor, the imitation of beauty, for real beauty. What is beauty, if it is not purity, radiance, and depth? The experience of love will activate our conscious and subconscious faculties. As our human nervous system develops, it will become a better instrument for sensing beauty. Its love, its relatedness, will grow.

Spirit is the Life that is behind everything. If we can love that Spirit, we will more and more find it in ourselves, in others, and in our surroundings, and we will take on its vivifying qualities.

DISCERNMENT

In the theater of our own experience we can come to discern the qualities of the Spirit from those of the compulsive ego. The ego is most concerned with its own survival, comfort, and vanity. It is the source of envy, resentment, pride, hypocrisy, guilt, and blame.

Spirit, on the other hand, is inwardly supportive, patient, forgiving, unconditionally generous, humble without being weak, and loving yet impartial. The individualized Spirit, which we call the soul, can learn to see beyond its immediate identifications in the material and psychological worlds.

Spirit possesses us; we don't possess it. We become aware of it and join with it. We become in Love with it. Eventually and incredibly, the ego, which had been such a tyrant, begins to lose its power and becomes a willing servant.

As we become familiar with Spirit, the material world—with all its diversity, with all that can be gained and lost—becomes secondary. It is not unimportant, but secondary in priority. We become less dependent on circumstances for our sense of well-being; we feel connected to Life and Spirit.

What may appear as a loss, for instance, in the material world is seen differently in the world of Spirit, where nothing can be lost. This does not mean that our grief just disappears—our losses remain. The sorrows of life embitter some and shatter others. Yet these same sorrows may set all of life against the backdrop of eternity and become a fountain of refreshment, a living energy to draw on. The agony of Jesus, the pain of Mary, and the submission of Muhammad are reminders that suffering cannot be avoided—and yet we are blessed.

The same Life that gave before will continue to give. We know and are aware that the Giver of Life, the Provider, the Generous One, the Beloved, can take any shape. People and events do not lose their significance; they become witnesses and evidence of Spirit, transparent to its radiance. We begin to see the qualities of the Creator in the creation. The heart is the manifesting part of the Spirit; it is activated through the unconditional love of life around us. Together with others we increase our life.

If it weren't for the presence of Spirit, this world would truly be a prison. But with Spirit and the faculty in humans that can perceive it, the world displays the infinite attributes of the One. Holy Spirit is everywhere.

ACTIVE CONTEMPLATION

What we contemplate, we become. Within our own Essence we discover the Infinite Being. The qualities that a pure attention perceives are sometimes not qualities that we have known as our own. We may discover great beauty in contemplation and yet not consider that beauty as originating with ourselves. It is said that "God is Beauty and loves the Beautiful." Love of beauty, especially spiritual Beauty, connects us to Spirit; our love of the One is a love of its beauty as known within our own Essence. This invisible beauty discovered within our own Self has a counterpart in the sensible world. The sensible world becomes beautiful to the extent that we are conscious of this invisible beauty within our Being.

We are awakened by a nostalgia that leads us beyond the world of appearances to new qualities contained within the heart. The qualities latent within our own Essence are Divine Attributes. It is because the Divine Compassion exists to reveal itself to us that there exists the possibility of knowing the Infinite by knowing ourselves and of knowing the particular Divine Attribute we most exemplify.

Why do we clutch the anonymity of our own nonbeing rather than awakening to real Being? Perhaps we will never fully understand the reason. The Divine Will appears to be faced with many obstacles. The Divine Compassion allows these obstacles to exist because the Perfected Human comes into existence through sacrifice and effort. There is no love where there is not polarity; it takes two to make One.

The Infinite One was a hidden treasure that longed to be known, and it created the seen and the unseen worlds in order that its treasure might be discovered. If we ask ourselves what this treasure contains, we might say the Divine Names, or Attributes of the One. We possess a faculty called the active imagination. If we are awake to the perfection of the moment we may begin to perceive directly what lies behind it, behind appearances and form. To be awake to the moment is to be awake to the Qualities that are manifesting through the moment. We know these Qualities because they are buried within our own subconscious mind, or heart.

Within the complete human being is a universe. Through knowing what a human being *is* we can determine the quality of our relationship to the wider universe.

The greater one's feeling, the greater the response from the universe, because the universe is infinite response. The greater one's intelligence (the awareness of interrelationships), the more intelligent the universe appears. It gives back to us what we give to it, only more so.

We have spiritual and intellectual freedom. Every point of view is possible; each has some validity and will in some way be affirmed by the universe, which comprises all possibilities. For someone who is rooted in despair, the universe will confirm despair. For those who love, serve, and remember, it will demonstrate corresponding values. What we love, we will become. Those who call on God with sincerity will find the living Presence of that God within themselves.

Love the Transformer

Love is recklessness, not reason.
Reason seeks a profit.
Love comes on strong, consuming herself,
    unabashed.

Yet in the midst of suffering
Love proceeds like a millstone,
hard-surfaced and straight-forward.

Having died to self-interest,
she risks everything and asks for nothing.
Love gambles away every gift God bestows.
             RUMI, *MATHNAWI*, VI, 1967–70

THE CREATIVE FORCE

"Never think of love as the goal of anything," a teacher of mine said, "always think of it as the cause." At all levels of existence a single cosmic energy is active. The whole universe is alive with intelligence, creativity, and constant evolution. Another name for this cosmic energy is Spirit, and we experience Spirit, this cosmic energy, as love. We prize Spirit wherever we find it—in a spirited horse or in anything else with spirit, life, and energy. At every stage of the Work we are increasing our awareness of it through gratitude and through particular exercises such as conscious breathing and sensing.

Because it is both attracting and creative, Spirit can also be described as fundamentally sexual. The charmed romances of adolescence have a spiritual quality; the devotions of a seeker in retreat may also be filled with the eagerness of someone on a first date.

Any creative act is an act of love. The Absolute Creator was the first to create out of Love, creating both the visible and the invisible worlds. The artist, the scientist, the craftsperson, the inventor—all to the extent that they are in love with their task—are creative.

This cosmic energy, which animates and vivifies, can be reflected at will by the human instrument, and our work is to make ourselves better reflectors of this Spirit. If we can learn the art of tapping cosmic energy at will, we will manifest more life, creativity, and love.

THE UNITING FORCE

Attraction operates at all levels within the electromagnetic field of existence. Electromagnetic, vibrational forces exist at the subatomic level. Energy is matter and matter is energy. At the chemical level elements such as carbon, hydrogen, and oxygen are attracted and form substances that enable organic life. Love is that fundamental creative and unifying power, an all-inclusive field.

At the level of human life there is eros, or love of the lovable. In its commonest form it is desire, wanting to possess. We want to make something our own, to consume it like those primitive people who would eat the heart of their enemy to acquire his power. We want to own land, a car, or a business. We want to exercise the power of our separate wills over other people and things. This is the level on which the individual ego operates. It represents a very limited and restrictive kind of love, but love nevertheless.

In its manifestation as sexual love, eros produces an intensity of feeling that can lead to the merging of two into one. The passion of this union is, however, all too short-lived, sometimes ending in the moments after physical satisfaction, or in most cases following a course of more gradual disenchantment.

Love is the tamer of ego. This is because it makes it possible for us to acknowledge for another the same significance and importance that we first attributed only to ourselves. That egoism that initially shaped our whole life encounters in love a living power that rescues it from its isolation and restores it to contact with something greater than itself.

The love of sharing, or *philos,* is less restrictive and limiting. We can see this phenomenon when people come together at a wedding, at a potluck meal, at the theater, at a horse race, in taverns, in cultural clubs, and in service organizations—in fact, in all the ways that people choose to share themselves. Through sharing love, a human being experiences itself as an independent and necessary organ of the whole of life. Together with others the individual's own significance becomes even more apparent.

Holistic, unconditional love, *agape,* is the unity in which duality disappears. It is as if a certain internal boundary has disappeared. With *agape* what we love is ourselves, the way a mother loves her child as herself. This is the meaning of loving another as oneself—transcending our phenomenal borders and experiencing ourselves in another and the other in, not apart from, us.

Eventually, if love is comprehensive, it unites us with everything and allows us to know that we *are* everything. Therefore how can we support the illusion of this isolated, separate self that is threatened by and defends itself from everything outside?

Love returns us to unity that is reality. Reality is not the isolation, suspicion, envy, selfishness, and fear of loss that we have come to take for granted; it is that we are all part of one life. The same Spirit moves in us all. You come to know this better when you realize that we all have the same kinds of feelings, the same wish to be known and respected, to share ourselves and let down our defenses.

We are continually faced with a choice between personal development, personal security, and comfort, on the one hand, and working for the whole and helping everyone and everything toward perfection, on the other. We are faced with a choice between looking out for our own good and contributing wholeheartedly to a common good. We are faced with focusing on self-love or increasing our love of all life.

When someone makes a loving gesture toward us, separation is bridged. When another human being welcomes you, showing you kindness and consideration, you feel at one with that person. Don't we wish to be at one with as many people as possible? It has been the dream of every major prophet to meld a people, created under the guidance of Divine Revelation, uniting them in respect, love, and surrender to the guidance of Truth.

When we are drawn into love, our own sense of an isolated, separate self melts. When you are in love and sit face-to-face with the one you love, you forget yourself in the beauty of your beloved. Because the beloved is a point of contact with Beauty, you are filled with this Beauty. Any lover becomes more beautiful through this love.

This Beloved, which most people know only in the first moment of romantic love, is in fact present in many faces and guises as our capacity for love grows. This capacity transforms us and makes us more alive. We are never so alive as when we are in love, so why should we restrict this love to the almost impossible conditions of romantic love? Can't we be lovers all the time?

THE TRANSFORMING FORCE

Love can be an act of will. People often ask, "But what if I don't feel it?" Because everything in cosmic existence is a two-way street, we can practice the fruits of love and through this invoke its reality. If we can manifest kindness, generosity, and patience, we will eventually discover the reality of love within ourselves. If we ever become transformed human beings, it will be because we have learned to fully love at will. Engendering a vibration of love can be our moment-to-moment conscious choice.

Love is not just attraction, nor is it even a high resonance. Its significance is that what begins as feeling produces actions in accord with that feeling. Love transforms copper into gold. The mistakes of lovers are better than righteous actions of the loveless. Even a bitter fruit from the hand of a beloved tastes sweet.

Lovers see what others do not, because being in love changes our state of consciousness, not only affecting how we feel and think but transforming even our sensuous perception. Love begets beauty, and beauty is our point of contact with love. Great artists are always, on some level, great lovers. Love will transform the ugly into the beautiful; it will see the beauty of anything. Once Muhammad came upon a mangy dog alongside the road. When he stopped his march to be with this poor animal, some of his companions commented on its ugliness. Muhammad pulled open the poor dog's mouth and said, "But don't you see? What beautiful teeth!"

Each person's love is different. We are temperamentally disposed to find and manifest love in different ways. Each individual heart has this love within and, at the same time, is drawn out into the electromagnetic field of life to those things, people, qualities, or situations that will spark this love. Our outer search is exposing to ourselves the love that is within, leading us to the point where we can recognize what we carry inside us. Nothing of value is accomplished without love, because it is the power that causes the heart to expand and embrace more and more.

Love is not the goal of anything; it is the cause of everything, including our own final transformation. Every human being's yearning to know and to relate is the action of love itself guiding us back to our own source. If we are faithful, it will transform us by connecting us to the highest qualities of the Spirit, which are the creative, life-giving qualities of love itself. It is the maker of true individuality, an individuality that finds its own greatest fulfillment in its communion with Spirit.

The Religion of Love

Without cause God gave us Being;
without cause give it back again.
Gambling yourself away is beyond any religion.

Religion seeks grace and favor,
but those who gamble these away are God's
    favorites,
for they neither put God to the test,
nor knock at the door of gain and loss.

RUMI, MATHNAWI, VI, 1971–74

Mevlana Jelaluddin Rumi has said, "The religion of Love is like no other." It has no form, and it is not dependent on laws, but it can be recognized despite outer forms by those who know it. It is the same religion that Jesus brought, calling it the "new covenant." The religion of Love was also brought by Muhammad and passed on through Ali and Abu Bakr to become Sufism. If we learn to love, we will not be visited by the coarseness against which the Law is meant to protect us. If we learn to be more in love, our behavior will be guided by a sense of appropriateness, which is the positive awareness of unity.

Self-righteousness is a disease of religion. Our work is to tame or melt the ego that separates us from Reality. The ego tells us that we are better or worse than other people, two false beliefs that are related. Perhaps we wouldn't feel the need to be better than others if we didn't suffer from the idea that we might not be as good as some others. The root of these feelings is comparison and abandonment of our trust in a Beneficent Reality. If we are too busy comparing ourselves to others, we are neglecting our real work of taming the ego that separates us from the One in all its forms. Compulsive thoughts comparing what we have and what we have attained with the holdings and achievements of others are thorns. How many times have we hurt ourselves or others on these thorns?

Just as a frightened and defensive animal is a dangerous animal, a weak person can be a dangerous person. We are weak when we are alone, and we are strong when we have Spirit as our friend. The more separate we are, the more frightened and defensive we are. The more people seem to be acting superior, putting themselves over others, the more insecure they are. Our work is to transform that insecurity, defensiveness, self-doubt, and fear into trust, goodwill, confidence, and courage.

Rumi said, "If your thought is a rose, you will be the rose garden." Here is a thought that is a rose: There is no strength except in Spirit. If the All-Powerful doesn't strengthen us, what strength do we have? If we depend on some protector other than the One, what protection do we have? If we love with some love other than Unconditional Love, what love do we have? Spirit has breathed itself into us. Why do we turn away from it rather than toward it? Why do we become frightened, selfish people, if not because we have turned away from this connection?

Do we need to feel superior to other people? What does that really feel like? Balancing on top of the telephone pole of ego brings only a moment's exhilaration and a lasting insecurity. Walking the straight and narrow path may be difficult and require our moment-by-moment awareness, but it brings with it a deep peace and a lasting feeling of having done the right thing.

And what about feeling unworthy, full of shame and self-pity? What does this have to do with humility? Humility is our sense of receiving everything from the One and submitting to its judgment and care. Humility is the innocence of being a child of Reality, of having Reality as our devoted mother and father. If we do not feel as if we have Reality as our parents, we must create it through finding the lost connection within us. Increasing this awareness and humility is available to us through knowing and understanding the religion of Love.

Religion is reverence. It has been brought by Abraham, by Jesus, and by Muhammad. We can find it in the Word and penetrate to its essence. Perhaps we shouldn't be too concerned with the forms if we haven't practiced the essentials. We can begin with humility, honesty, generosity, patience, kindness, and goodwill. All the religious rituals and esoteric sciences exist to serve these fundamental virtues and not as an end in themselves. If we use these rituals and sciences to support our self-importance, we are hurting ourselves. If we remember humility, honesty, generosity, patience, kindness, and goodwill, we will be serving the Beneficent Reality and the true religion of Oneness. We will be the rose garden.

GIFTS FOR THE SHAIKH

We traveled to Konya, Turkey, with two young boys, five and two, during a period of martial law. Arriving in Konya we took a taxi directly to Shaikh Suleyman Dede's house, where there was no phone, not knowing whom we would find there.

The neighborhood was a quiet, bare street of mud-walled one- and two-story buildings. We passed a large cemetery beyond which rose a minaret. The cab driver dropped us off in front of a small alley and pointed us down it. Turning the corner of the alley we were faced with a wooden gate-door, which we unlatched, and entered a patio around which were placed rosebushes in metal cans. Inside a large glass window we could see Dede sitting cross-legged on a divan in his pajamas. Whatever apprehension we had melted as we saw him and he motioned for us to come inside. We had brought some red gladioluses because we hadn't been able to find roses at the flower shop. I took a picture of Dede, my wife, Camille, and my two-year-old son offering the flowers within minutes of our arrival, and that picture shows Dede's beauty as much as any other I have seen. Here we had returned to our home; here, even without a common language to speak, we entered deep into conversation.

We left that day with plans for Dede to meet us at our hotel at eight the next morning and then to "meet Mevlana," as he put it. I made a point of getting to the lobby fifteen minutes early so that I could pay for the cab as he arrived. In my naïveté I never thought that an eighty-year-old man with a serious hernia would walk a few miles to meet us. He was already sitting quietly in the lobby awaiting us. In answer to a previous inquiry, the desk clerk started to tell me that there was nowhere I could send our laundry, which had accumulated during our travels, but that one of their staff could do it for a price greater than what our room was costing. When Dede caught the gist of our conversation, he said that he would take our laundry to do at home. Of course, I wouldn't give it to him, because the idea of an elderly couple doing our laundry was ridiculous to me, even without yet being aware that they had no washing machine.

Dede was always like this—quick to be aware of needs, giving more than getting. We would try to find ways to give, bringing things whenever we visited, but we felt we couldn't give enough. If we brought Dede and his wife a bag of oranges, we would have to leave with two watermelons under our arm. I can see now that there is so much more that I could have given, but didn't know how to. I was still learning how to receive.

Someone once told me the story of how after staying with Dede and Ferishta, his wife, when his day of departure arrived, Dede rose in the early morning hours and set about to buy some of the twenty-six ingredients that make Asura, a special mixture of dried fruit, nuts, and grains, *which according to tradition is the food that Noah prepared the day he sighted land. My friend was amazed that there was anyone so spontaneously and naturally good.*

I said that we were lucky to have met a man like Dede.

"It's not a matter of luck," he said.

Someone I know once watched Suleyman Dede leave a room through a certain door, appearing so small that he seemed to become nothing to go through it. Hearing this reminded me of the words "God is so humble, he totally hides himself within creation."

Worship: Contact With the Infinite

Water says to the dirty, "Come here."
The dirty one says, "I am so ashamed."
Water says,
"How will your shame be washed away without
  me."

RUMI, *MATHNAWI*, II, 1366–67

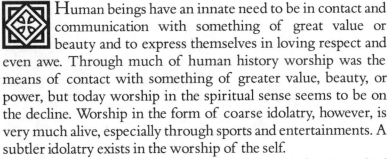 Human beings have an innate need to be in contact and communication with something of great value or beauty and to express themselves in loving respect and even awe. Through much of human history worship was the means of contact with something of greater value, beauty, or power, but today worship in the spiritual sense seems to be on the decline. Worship in the form of coarse idolatry, however, is very much alive, especially through sports and entertainments. A subtler idolatry exists in the worship of the self.

When it is said that there are no gods but God, it is implied that we shall worship the only God, that we shall recognize the Beneficent Reality behind the forms and events of our lives. Idolatry, in any form, is the fundamental sin, that which separates us from the Real. When we make an idol of the self, we increase self-will, self-justification, self-righteousness, and self-indulgence. Our idolatries include ambition, greed, misplaced sexual desire, the compulsive needs for intoxication and stimulation, and the need for attention. Whatever commands our attention is our master; whatever we worship consciously or unconsciously is what we serve.

If we value something more than Spirit it is because of a misapprehension, a narrowness of vision. If we are identified with our small, partial self, we will be captured in the net of desires, whereas if we are identified with Spirit, what we desire will be the desire of Wholeness.

Worship in its original sense means "to value," or consider something worthy. The word is associated mainly with religious acts, and especially with those performed by some religious authority, such as a priest. In reality, however, every person who prays, who makes a call to Higher Reality, is performing an act of worship and stands as the equivalent of a priest.

The One Being is not outside ourselves, not separate from anyone. Absolute Being allowed the way for everything to exist. This Being is present within us as a nondimensional point. To understand this we must first create an inner vacuum, free of the pressures of conventional beliefs, of personal compulsions, and of duality and separation. This pure vacuum will show us the withinness of the One. In worship we allow ourselves to be harmonized by something of the highest value. The regular and patterned exercise of consciousness, the energy of remembrance within worship, is a basic need. In worship we are more likely to experience a correspondence between body and soul, behavior and feeling, because we are calling on a harmonizing power.

Two qualities that are said to be necessary to worship and prayer are recollection and humility. We begin by recollecting ourselves and asking something of this nondimensional point that is our contact with Spirit. We gather the whole of ourselves into a single sincere act, calling upon this slumbering spiritual essence within us in order that it may be activated and respond. The individual mind can make contact with the greater Mind dormant within us.

With humility, which is the awareness of our dependence on the One, we will be opened to a spiritual inflow. Our own self will become transparent to the light that is meant to shine through and from us. Humility allows the annihilation of what is less real about us and the reflection of what is more real. Through worship, a loving attunement, we better reflect Spirit. We can learn to do it more and more at will.

We come face-to-face with Love as we gather in its name. Love is the milieu in which we all exist. Together we can join our hearts to this field. We elevate ourselves through the spiritual energy accumulated by individuals together, gathering ourselves, remembering our true dependency on the One. All we need is within if we are free of the obstructing ego. Only the ego can separate us from the One. We can enter the Kingdom of Heaven by arriving at the simplicity of a child. Our egos can be transformed into servants and procure for us our passport to the infinite life.

A protective grace becomes available to those who share worship. With this grace perception changes. We develop by opening ourselves to every manifestation of life we encounter. As we open ourselves, the Divine Milieu pours in. With a strong enough love, we can make the journey of life without fear, becoming invulnerable.

When we gather our faculties, giving them both direction and stillness, as if before the face of Love, we are also preparing ourselves to remember this Love spontaneously at other times. If we consistently direct our attention, desire, will, thought, and feeling in the direction of Love, the Love thus realized becomes a vital power and capacity. Through worship we are rejoined with the One we worship.

Of all the human activities that I am acquainted with, worship, provided it is with presence, is the most direct route toward contact with the Infinite. Worship in communion with others is even more fruitful than worship alone, provided one can find a community of lovers. Worship that includes the whole of us is vastly more effective than worship that includes only a part of us. Worship can begin in stillness of mind, heart, and body, leading to an inner activation, a deep recollection in which we make a spontaneous and specific call to the Spirit within, asking of it all the qualities and strengths we need to serve in life. This spontaneous prayer can be clear and resonant, since through the voice it is possible to awaken the dormant essence within ourselves and others. Worship may include conscious breathing, chanting, singing, and movement. It need not be in a church, nor should it be afflicted with religiosity, piousness, or sentimentality. Worship may yet take forms that are entirely new and creative, for what is of Spirit *is* creative.

Refining the Psyche

The five spiritual senses are all connected.
They've grown from one root.
As one grows strong, the others strengthen, too:
each one becomes a cupbearer to the rest.
Seeing with the eye increases speech;
speech increases discernment in the eye.
As sight deepens, it awakens every sense,
so that perception of the spiritual
becomes familiar to them all.

RUMI, *MATHNAWI*, II, 3236–39

A friend had taken my family out into the ocean on his sailboat. He had introduced me to a new navigational system that allowed him to know within yards his exact position on earth. Electromagnetic waves were beamed back and forth between the sea and a satellite in outer space. What an extraordinary sign of the capabilities of the human intellect! It occurred to me that the human being also has just this sort of equipment but that it has been shut off by some accident. There was a time when men of the sea operated by subtle instincts, sensing location, weather, and movement. Now this operation has been computerized to the point where the great oil tankers have an alarm that is supposed to sound if they come within miles of the coast. However, the alarms don't always work, and these ships sometimes run aground.

We have subtle subconscious faculties we are not using. Beyond the limited analytical intellect is a vast realm of mind that includes psychic and extrasensory abilities; intuition; wisdom; a sense of unity; aesthetic, qualitative, and creative faculties; and image-forming and symbolic capacities. Though these faculties are many, we give them a single name with some justification, because they are operating best when they are in concert. They comprise a mind, moreover, in spontaneous connection to the Cosmic Mind. This total mind we call "heart."

The word *heart* has a specific meaning in our spiritual glossary. The heart includes those faculties that are beyond the intellect; but as long as we are attached to this physical body, we are working *through* the intellect. In the process of translation the intellect transforms the subtle perceptions of the psyche into recognizable, familiar images and thoughts. The intellect may give the final expression of these faculties, acting as translator and analyzer, but nothing originates with the intellect; it rearranges known elements, categorizes, and compares. Sometimes the intellect does this in an elegant and purposeful way; other times it makes false connections or reduces new information to old concepts, functioning in a mechanical, habitual manner. The art of intentional psychic functioning depends on the ability to accurately translate subtle perceptions as they emerge from the subconscious into consciousness.

LEVEL OF MIND

The heart is that antenna that receives the emanations of subtler levels of existence. The human heart has its proper field of function beyond the limits of the superficial, reactive ego-self. Awakening the heart, or the spiritualized mind, is an unlimited process of making the mind more sensitive, focused, energized, subtle, and refined, of joining it to its cosmic milieu, the infinity of love.

We can trace the development of spiritual awareness in terms of the levels of mind. An ordinary human being of our time and culture lives within the limits of his or her social and familial conditioning. Our experience is in our thoughts and emotions. These occupy our so-called conscious mind, that narrow slit of awareness that is easily filled with particular thoughts and feelings. This mind is not truly conscious—i.e., transcendently aware—but is the focal point of a limited awareness. The mind is operating at the level of automatic functioning much of the time and occasionally at the level of sensitive functioning, noticing and dealing with change.

It is a mind filled with associations, influenced by unconscious beliefs, compulsions, and contradictions, but it can seldom discriminate between these unconscious forces and the deeper prompting of the heart. Insofar as this conscious mind is a slave to unexamined likes and dislikes and egotistical impulses, it cannot see into or connect to its own depths. It sees everything through the distortions of its desires and thinks as a result of them. It experiences emotions according to whether these desires are satisfied or frustrated. Mentally it operates through associations, concepts, categories, stereotypes, preconceptions, and so forth. It doesn't see the forest for the trees, and the trees are not seen for what they are but as things on which it projects its expectations, concepts, and neediness.

At the beginning of spiritual work, and for as long as it takes, it is necessary to go through a process of deconditioning: meticulously observing the influences of our conditioning, learning more and more to see things as they are. Simultaneously, it is necessary to cultivate the sensitive and conscious capacities. Now trees become trees. Now, too, we can perhaps see the forest. Now an "isness" or "suchness" comes through, because we are consciously aware. We have deconditioned the mind of associations and egotistic projections and reconditioned it through conscious awareness, which allows a direct perception and communion. This, however, is not the final stage, because although we have become more conscious, we are not yet functioning with all our subconscious faculties.

When these faculties are available to the mind, meaning and value flood into consciousness. We not only see trees as they are, but we perceive them as the embodiment of qualities and meaning. The difference between the Meaning that is experienced from the subconscious mind, or heart, and the meaning that is projected when the mind is at the stage of lower self, or ego, is this: heart knowledge is living and creative, while ego is repetitive and predictable.

When the subconscious faculties are awakened, the human inheritance can be awakened to its maximum. An awakened human being begins to live in contact with and work in cooperation with the Creative Power.

ACTIVATION OF THE SUBCONSCIOUS FACULTIES

How much of the latent capacities of the mind do we employ? How often are we conscious, actively receptive, living in true service, or asking a real question? How often do we listen within, and how often do we consciously receive the subtle impressions of the heart? On the other hand, how much time do we give to keeping our mundane accounts, imagining an imaginary future, reliving a limited past, scheming to get more of this or that, to prevent this or that loss, judging, blaming, and worrying?

The subconscious mind is tapped in a myriad of ways. A creative artist, through discipline, craft, and surrender, can tap into it. Any men or women of knowledge can tap into it by proper preparation, by becoming familiar with the knowledge of their field and then framing what they need to know with a true question. A psychic may select a target and gather impressions from the subconscious. Those whose yearning is wisdom must listen within for the subconscious to yield its secrets.

One of the ways that knowledge is available to us is through our subconscious faculties. Within the mirror of our own awareness, however, we experience a concatenation of impressions that include immediate sense impressions, emotional reactions, mental associations, and memories, as well as the subtle perceptions that hover right at the threshold of consciousness.

Our subtle, subconscious faculties are operating to some degree whether we are consciously aware of them or not. We may unconsciously follow or disregard these subtle perceptions, depending on the degree of our own compulsiveness or rational resistance. We can, however, learn to integrate them into our daily life if we practice acting on them and receiving feedback from those actions. Gradually, we will learn through our own experience how to trust this level of knowledge that is beyond reason and the senses.

The ability to use our subconscious faculties depends on a quality of presence that is not too disturbed by the more superficial levels of our subjective experience and can discriminate the different levels of impressions. If awareness is dominated by any of the coarser impressions—by thought, desire, environmental impressions, or other forms of mental noise—it cannot catch those subtle and fleeting impressions of the subconscious.

With the development of presence comes a more refined awareness of all levels of experience. If, for instance, we know how we feel, think, and perceive when we are near a certain kind of person or place, we will be better able to interpret those subtle impressions that refer to people or places at a distance. The more we are conscious, the more our own mirror of awareness can reflect knowledge and information less restricted by space and time.

We should learn to be cautious about accepting images that arrive fully formed and detailed, since these are likely to be creations of memory and association. We should also be wary of information or impressions that come too quickly and strongly, since these are more likely to be examples of mental noise. Generally, the information coming through our subtle perceptions will gradually fill out the picture. This is different from the information that arrives prefabricated and clear. It is more likely that in the authentic functioning of our subtle faculties a wholeness will emerge through the accumulation of sometimes fleeting and spontaneous impressions.

Whether we are talking about psychic perception, artistic creation, or the search for wisdom, certain similarities present themselves when the subconscious faculties begin to work. A good poet must recognize the difference between the metaphor that is an easy cliché and the one that has an unexpected quality of appropriateness. The psychic must recognize the difference between an image that comes from the personal subconscious— from memory or association—and the impression that is surprising and carries the feeling that the target is being contacted. As this begins to happen, a spectrum of subtle impressions may be received that include sensual, emotional, and other kinds of information. Often there will be a sense of emotional involvement with what is being received. The artist will have a peculiar sense of being "on." The seeker of wisdom may find that the knowledge found within affects the feelings profoundly and may even be accompanied by visions, celestial sounds, or delightful fragrances.

The impressions we receive from our subconscious faculties will go through some form of translation into conscious awareness and perhaps a further translation into some concrete form. Whether this translation is visual, musical, literary, or intellectual, our skillfulness will be tested by the degree to which we distort, edit, or embellish what we receive. With practice and experience we can learn to focus on significant details and select from the whole spectrum of impressions that which best conveys the uniqueness of the subject.

So far I have been talking about the intentional application of subtle faculties. But the spontaneous reception of knowledge and guidance is at least as important in our spiritual life. If we accept that which our own selves can will and be conscious of is a tiny fragment of the Whole, then we must humbly accept the guidance and promptings that are given to us by higher sources. The higher sources, however, cannot communicate with us when all our channels are filled with coarser preoccupations and when our own awareness is not in a receptive state. To receive the spiritual guidance that will allow us to be of service, to be at the right place at the right time with the right means, to be a full participant in life, we will need a presence, a clarity, an openness.

Simultaneous with this presence, a loving attitude toward all manifestations of life will help create the necessary invisible connections. The most striking examples of spontaneous psychic experience are those in which a loved one is involved in some danger. The most accurate psychic information is received when there is an emotional involvement with the subject. The greatest artistic creations are produced by those whose love of beauty is profound. The greatest advances in science—and Einstein's work is an example of this—are those made with a great love of knowing the universe. In all these examples, love is the means.

All authentic spiritual traditions teach us to be unconcerned with psychic performance for its own sake, but this should not prevent us from recognizing the principles of subtle perception and the fact that these perceptions are our birthright.

COMING UNDER THE PROTECTIVE GRACE OF LOVE

We spiritualize the mind by freeing it from the domination of its superficial and ego-bound preoccupations. When the mind is dominated and controlled by habits of desire, negative emotions, passive imagination, opinions, and concepts, it is cut off from the wisdom of the subconscious, which is its link with the Cosmic Mind. Spiritualizing the mind allows the individual psyche to be attuned with the milieu and energy of love, to better resonate with the Cosmic Mind.

The heart perceives the Spirit that moves in everything and apprehends the soul of each thing. This is because everything in existence is the manifestation of a single Source: the Absolute Divine Unknown. This Absolute in motion is called Spirit, which is experienced as love in its many subtleties. When Spirit has taken any kind of form, that form has its own soul. The heart opens to the Spirit-content that is in everything, and this causes the heart to become more subtle and more pervasive.

As the heart is refined, as we develop our latent human faculties, we more and more come under the protective grace of love. Without this action of love on the mind, the individual psyche would remain as something separate and autonomous. Through the creative and attractive power of love, the mind is helped to make contact with more and more of the universe, to feel its participation in the continuing miracle of existence.

What in religious language might be called the satanic qualities are the product of this isolation and contraction from the milieu of love, the contraction being ego. The egoistic mind, of course, reaches a dead end in its refinement. It may awaken some of its latent human potential, but it does not reach completion, because its lack of love has cut it off from its ecology, from the Whole. It knows itself as a part rather than the Whole.

To open in love to other beings is to put ourselves under the protection of Love. The thing we are protected from is the tyranny of our own ego. In the presence of love, the tyrannical ego either flees in terror or becomes less of a threat and more of a servant.

The preparations for transforming the mind may include fasting and other forms of purification. Special techniques of conscious breathing, sound, rhythm, or color visualization may be used to concentrate energy in the nervous system. This purification and strengthening of the nervous system is a prerequisite for resonating with the Cosmic Mind.

Another prerequisite is a sincere heart contact with a source of guidance in the invisible world. While it is possible to have this contact without knowing or intending it, the preferred way is to know consciously from where this help comes. In some indigenous cultures shamans, for instance, contact a nature spirit or power animal. A greater potential is offered by having an enlightened being, a master or a prophet, as a point of contact. This point of contact is of value only because its content is the same as the Divine content. A being who has realized unity with Spirit is like a harbor through which one enters the ocean. A harbor, bay, or gulf, however, is not other than the ocean; it is simply a more accessible approach.

DISSOLVING

The mind can be understood as a substance that can exist in various states, just as H_2O can exist as ice, water, steam, vapor, and humidity. As ice its solidity limits it, and it must follow the physical laws of a solid; as water it can flow. As humidity, however, it exists in a subtle, interpenetrating state, occupying a much greater expanse.

I noticed and experienced for myself this level of being clearly through my teacher. In Dede's presence I felt at one with him, and through him at one with everything. We were not practicing this as an explicit exercise, but for me the result of contact with such a human being was that I dissolved. The same functional me, who could cut wood or edit a manuscript, existed, but some part of myself had dissolved and yet was still present. I would take a walk from the farm where we were staying deeper into the country or in the direction of town, and both experiences were equally soaked with Spirit. Then it occurred to me that this state was like sugar dissolving in water. The sugar, which was me, had become invisible, and yet it was there; it could be tasted. When I returned to my teacher, all I could say was, "Thanks for helping me to dissolve like sugar in water."

As these things begin to happen, the conventional idea of self begins to break down. The boundaries of the self are less limited, and yet the identity has not been weakened. The self has dissolved: It is there, but not in its old form. A new quality enters into our relationships—a deeper love, as if we were loving a part of ourselves. Within ourselves we are surrounded by presences; the saints and masters are here within us, as is the Presence of Spirit.

The individual mind that we spiritualize is not something separate from the mind of the universe, but a reflection of this mind experienced through the vehicle of the nervous system and its subtle centers. The heart is the individualized, manifesting part of the Cosmic Mind. It is a reflection of this Cosmic Mind's attributes: love, compassion, mercy, patience, generosity, will, service, creativity, beauty, wisdom, awareness, and innumerable other qualities. To the extent that we can increase our reflection of these qualities, we are also developing the heart.

Service Within
the Divine Unknown

Each moment contains
a hundred messages from God:
To every cry of "Oh Lord,"
He answers a hundred times, "I am here."

RUMI, *MATHNAWI*, VI, 1578

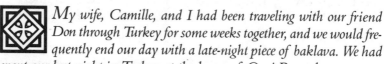 *My wife, Camille, and I had been traveling with our friend Don through Turkey for some weeks together, and we would frequently end our day with a late-night piece of baklava. We had spent our last night in Turkey at the home of Oruj Bey, where we sang Sufi Illahis and various people played instruments until the early hours of the morning. On our way back to our hotel, we were feeling very light and energized as we almost floated through the back streets of Istanbul. The city was quiet and there was no one on the streets except for an occasional soldier with an automatic rifle. I was carrying a copy of* The Ruins of the Heart, *which I had intended to give to Mehmet, a rug dealer near the Istanbul bazaar who had expressed an interest in the book. We would be leaving for the airport in the morning, before Mehmet's shop would open. I still wanted to give him the book, but I didn't know how this would be possible.*

The three of us were walking down a broad avenue not far from the

bazaar when I saw a lone figure standing about a block ahead, his back toward us. From a distance it looked like Mehmet. As we drew near to him the figure turned around, and it was he.

"Salaam Aleikhoum," I said. "Here is a book that I wanted you to have."

"Thank you, brother, I am pleased to have it. Would you care to join me at my uncle's shop? The shop is closed, but He has just finished baking tomorrow's baklava."

When we are aware of the abundance of life, synchronous events unfold in the continuum of time; love brings together what needs to be brought together. Often in the Middle East my companions and I would find ourselves more clearly in that space of imminent meaning and grace.

The psyche's refinement toward a deeper and more continuous presence results in our being able to meet more and more manifestations of Life with unconditional Love. We are able to overcome our separation to such an extent that we feel at one with more and more. Our awareness of our connection with Life increases our sensitivity to our environment and awakens us to more and more opportunities for service, interaction, and cross-fertilization; we find that our needs are met as well, and the circle continues. In every moment our environment presents us with needs. Our service is the natural outcome—one could almost say the mechanical consequence—of our awareness of our environment as a whole and our connection with the Creative Power.

If we find that we are incapable of meeting life with unconditional love, we can at least begin to practice shifting awareness from the preoccupation with ourselves to a wider field of awareness, including the needs of those around us. As we become accustomed to this shift, opportunities for service arise often and naturally. But service without presence is sleep, and if we are identified with service, if we expect thanks or some reward, it instead becomes a demand.

It is good to do what is right and to feel good about it. It is good to serve those whom we love. It is necessary to contribute to the general welfare through generous and public-spirited action. All of this is basic to a decent human life, but it is not yet at the level of spiritual practice.

The service that is spiritual practice is beyond attraction and beyond the limited ego. This service depends on a shift of awareness. Through it we are lifted out of our egoism; in it we become motivated by unconditional love of the life around us. It is the Beloved loving through us and the Generous giving through us. Even anger and criticism can be welcomed when it is from the Beloved, while even the help and praise of those who "serve" with arrogance or self-righteousness feels like a poison to us. We do not want it, even if we need it.

Service is the outcome of our awareness of the environment as a whole. When we shift from our personal preoccupations to a wider awareness, and when we have overcome the inner tyrannies of attraction and preference, we can be more awake to opportunities for service. We can begin to be in the right place at the right time to fill a need.

Any action without presence is mechanical, and any step outward requires a corresponding step inward. If we are to truly grow in service, we must simultaneously grow in presence. The more our inner faculties are engaged, the more service will come naturally.

As the psyche opens in love to its milieu, a marriage occurs between the heart and the electromagnetic milieu of love, and a child is born: will, or conscious action. Until then we have only ego—the bastard child of intellect and desire. The marriage of the subtle faculties of mind, or the heart, with unconditional love gives birth to the true, conscious, unqualified will. The quality of action at this level of human functioning is creative and holistic. The soul has the possibility to act from its own initiative and in the name of love, not merely to react from personal desire and insecurity. Since the refined psyche extends far beyond the phenomenal self, its actions have a magnetic, even a miraculous, quality. An example of this is Mother Theresa's visit to Beirut during the fighting there. She said, before going, that on the day of her visit the fighting would stop. She did not demand that the fighting stop, but it did.

UNCONDITIONING

This merging of the heart with the milieu of Love brings us to the stage known as unconditioning, which is the highest state of subtlety of the mind and heart. The subtle faculties become so expansive and all-embracing that we see our own Self in everything. The identity becomes so expansive that it feels its union with Divine Being. It is as if the human being were a pole, with individuality at one end and the Divine Being at the other.

Through learning to love we come to a perception of the deeper dimensions present in the real world. Love is no longer merely a form of attraction, nor is it some virtuous sentiment that improves the character. It is the cause of everything and the electromagnetic milieu in which we live. Wherever we find love, it will lead us farther along the path of Return to the Source of Love.

Shaihk Abdulla Ansari, an Afghani teacher of the eleventh century, gave these answers to three fundamental questions: What is worship? To realize reality. What is the sacred law? To do no evil. What is reality? Selflessness. His answers convey a profound and universal meaning, free of cultural conditioning, religious dogmatism, and sentimentality.

Metaphysicians may think about reality and what it might essentially be, refining their formulations for logical consistency and linguistic resonance. While the metaphysician only thinks about reality, we can remember to *be* that reality. We can be instantaneously within Spirit. Everything happens within a matrix of Spirit; everything is ordered and lawful. Knowing this helps us to feel our connection with a guiding Creative Power.

Sometimes we have to slow down to make that connection. Some people take a second to slow down, while some take a lifetime. If you have confidence that you can make that connection—in motion, in relationship—you should try. But don't deceive yourself; the connection is subtle.

Perhaps we have gone for many years *toward* Reality. Why shouldn't we accept that we are *within* it right now? If we are within it,. what is there to worry about? Isn't Reality fundamentally compassionate and merciful? Isn't apparent chaos just a thin veil over Order?

Yet we allow ourselves to be separated through our unconscious resistance. We become absorbed in our illusions and fantasies—our petty negativities, jealousies, insecurities, resistances, judgments, doubts, and vanities. Can we overcome our resistance to waking up? Can we recognize the extent to which we are living under the tyranny of the false self, and at the same time awaken to the living presence in the heart of the human being?

A sigh of compassion is within this world. The Divine Unknown is nearer to us than our jugular vein. Its face is everywhere to be seen; Its qualities surround us. Everything is being breathed out of the silence of Spirit. This is the key to the secrets of the moment, to the fullness of living. Let it breathe us; let us be this Living Presence.

What Sufism Is

Sufism is a way of life in which a deeper identity is discovered and lived. This deeper identity, or essential Self, is beyond the already known personality and is in harmony with everything that exists. It has abilities of awareness, action, creativity, and love that are far beyond those of the superficial personality. Eventually it is understood that these abilities belong to a greater Being that we each individualize in our own unique way while never being separate from it.

Sufism is less a doctrine or a belief system than an experience and a way of life. It is a tradition of enlightenment that carries the essential truth forward through time. Tradition, however, must be conceived in a vital and dynamic sense. Its expression must not remain limited to the religious and cultural forms of the past. The truth of Sufism requires reformulation and fresh expression in every age.

This does not mean that Sufism will compromise its challenge to a stubbornly materialistic society. It is and will remain a critic of worldliness—by which is meant everything that causes us to be forgetful of the Divine Reality. It is and must be a way out of the labyrinth of a bankrupt materialistic culture. Most important, however, it is an invitation to meaningfulness and well-being.

Sufism, as we know it, developed within the cultural matrix of Islam. The Islamic revelation presented itself as the latest expression of the essential message brought to humanity by the prophets of all ages. The Qur'an recognizes the validity of 120,000 prophets, or messengers, who have come to awaken us from our selfish egoism and remind us of our spiritual nature. It confirmed the validity of past revelations, while asserting that the original message was often distorted over the course of time.

Sufism's claim to universality is founded on the broad recognition that there is only one God, the God of all people and all true religions. Sufism understands itself to be the wisdom realized by the great prophets—explicitly including Jesus, Moses, David, Solomon, and Abraham, among others, and implicitly including other unnamed enlightened beings of every culture.

In the Western world today diverse groups exist under the name of Sufism. On the one hand, there are those who would say that no true Sufism can exist without the appreciation and practice of the principles of Islam. On the other, some groups more or less ignore the Islamic roots of Sufism and take their teaching from farther downstream, from Sufis who may or may not have had contact with specifically Islamic teachings. Furthermore, there are those who accept Sufism as both form and essence, while there are others who are Sufi in essence but not in form. In my opinion, an appreciation and understanding of the Qur'an, the sayings of Muhammad, and historical Sufism is invaluable to the wayfarer on the Sufi path.

Historically, Sufism was not conceived as separate from the essence of Islam. Its teachers all traced their enlightenment through a chain of transmission going back to Muhammad. While they may have disagreed with certain interpretations of Islam, they never questioned the essential validity of the Qur'anic revelation, nor were they fundamentalists in the sense of rigidly interpreting that revelation or discrediting other faiths. Most often they represented the highest achievements within Islamic culture and were a force of tolerance and moderation.

Over fourteen centuries the broad Sufi tradition has contributed a body of literature second to none on earth. Somehow the guiding principles of the Qur'an, and the heroic virtue of Muhammad and his companions provided an impetus that allowed a spirituality of love and consciousness to flourish. Those who follow the Sufi path today are the inheritors of an immense treasure of wisdom and literature.

Beginning from its roots at the time of Muhammad, Sufism has organically grown like a tree with many branches. The cause of the branching has usually been the appearance of an enlightened teacher whose methods and contributions to the teaching have been enough to initiate a new line of growth. These branches generally do not see one another as rivals. A Sufi, in some cases, may be initiated into more than one branch in order to receive the grace (*baraka*) and knowledge of particular orders.

There is little cultishness in the work of Sufis. Sufis of one order may, for instance, visit the gatherings of another. Even the charisma of a particular teacher is always viewed from the perspective that this gift is owed entirely to God. The charisma is valuable insofar as it may bind the hearts of students to a human being who represents the truth of the teaching, but many safeguards exist to remind everyone that personality worship and inordinate pride in one's affiliation are forms of idolatry, a great sin.

If Sufism recognizes one central truth, it is the unity of being, that we are not separate from the Divine. This is a truth that our age is in an excellent position to appreciate—emotionally, because of the shrinking of our world through communications and transportation, and intellectually, because of developments in modern physics. We are One: one people, one ecology, one universe, one being. If there is a single truth, worthy of the name, it is that we are all integral to the Truth, not separate. The realization of this truth has its effects on our sense of who we are, on our relationships to others and to all aspects of life. Sufism is about realizing the current of love that runs throughout all life, the unity behind forms.

If Sufism has a central method, it is the development of presence and love. Only presence can awaken us from our enslavement to the world and our own psychological processes, and only cosmic love can comprehend the Divine. Love is the highest activation of intelligence, for without it nothing great would be accomplished, whether spiritually, artistically, socially, or scientifically.

Sufism is the attribute of those who love. Lovers are people who are purified by love, free of themselves and their own qualities and fully attentive to the Beloved. This is to say that Sufis are not held in bondage by any quality of their own because they see everything they are and have as belonging to the Source. An early Sufi, Shebli, said: "The Sufi sees nothing except God in the two worlds."

This book is about one aspect of Sufism: presence, and how this presence can be developed and used to activate our essential human qualities. Abu Muhammad Muta'ish says: "The Sufi is he whose thought keeps pace with his foot, i.e. he is entirely present: his soul is where his body is, and his body where his soul is, and his soul where his foot is, and his foot where his soul is. This is the sign of presence without absence. Others say on the contrary: 'He is absent from himself but present with God.' It is not so: he is present with himself and present with God."

We live in a culture that has been described as materialistic, alienating, neurotically individualistic, narcissistic, and yet ridden with anxiety, shame, and guilt. From the Sufi point of view, humanity today is suffering under the greatest tyranny, the tyranny of the ego. We worship innumerable false idols, but all of them are forms of the ego.

There are many ways for the human ego to usurp even the purest spiritual values. The true Sufi is the one who makes no claims to virtue or truth, but who lives a life of presence and self-less love. More important than what we believe is how we live. If certain beliefs lead to exclusiveness, self-righteousness, and fanaticism, it is the vanity of the believer that is the problem. If the remedy increases the sickness, an even more basic remedy is called for.

The idea of presence with love may be the most basic remedy for the prevailing materialism, selfishness, and unconsciousness of our age. In our obsession with our false selves, in turning our backs on God, we have also lost our essential Self, our own divine spark. In forgetting God, we have forgotten ourselves. Remembering God is the beginning of remembering ourselves.

Glossary

As a special glossary develops around the needs of any profession, the discipline of awakening also has terms that reflect its special needs. The following definitions will help to reveal and clarify certain understandings that emerge from a holistic grasp of human possibilities. A glossary is one way of not only clarifying but also concentrating knowledge. A careful reading of this section is highly recommended.

ABUNDANT LIFE: the result of consciously becoming whole with mind, body, soul, and ecology.

APPROPRIATENESS: the child of love and humbleness.

ATTAINMENT: the progress in using human faculties. Something is an attainment if it can be used at will.

AWARENESS: any perception. *Aware* is not necessarily synonymous with *conscious* as defined in this book.

BEAUTY: anything that becomes our point of contact with love.

BEING: the creative potential or Essence behind existence; the "is-ness" that contains all potential qualities.

BELOVED: our point of contact with Essence. The Beloved can be a person, and it can be everywhere.

CENTERS: capacities of the human nervous system to reflect the one Creative Energy. For example, the brain is the center of the intellectual mind; other more subtle faculties exist, which in Sufism are called *latifas* (subtleties).

CHARISMA: the ability of putting into action the Divine attributes of the psyche; Divine charm.

CONSCIOUSNESS: the degree of our awareness, inner and outer, on as many levels of experience as possible; a comprehensive awareness that encompasses thinking, feeling, and bodily sensation without being limited by them.

CONTENTMENT: an awareness of one's present richness without precluding more.

DISCIPLINE: methodical pursuit; the state of someone who acts with a purpose.

EGO: the conscious mind, as distinguished from the subconscious mind; "I."

EMANCIPATION: freedom from the fear of loss.

ESSENCE: 1. God; that from which everything proceeds. 2. the essential nature of anything; that which is inherently and utilizably good in anything.

ESSENTIAL SELF: the Higher Self; that in ourselves which is in contact with the Creative Power, or Cosmic Mind.

FAITH: hope substantiated by knowledge.

FALSE SELF: the self-righteousness of the intellect working for its own survival at the expense of the whole Self; the illegitimate child of the affair between intellect and desire.

FREEDOM: 1) the result of greater presence. 2) the state of having will. 3) psychologically, being free of negativity.

GATHERING: collecting all of ourselves of which we are aware to our "I."

GOD: the absolute source and subtlest state of everything; Essence, the Creative Power, the Cosmic Mind.

GRACE: the continuous overflowing of the Divine Essence, which is coming to all. The grace we receive depends on our ability to receive it.

GRASP: understanding attained through mobilizing our conscious and subconscious minds, as well as our five senses.

HEART: the subconscious/superconscious mind; all the subtle faculties that are nonintellectual.

HUMAN BEING: that part of nature which has evolved to be the most complete reflector of Spirit within this material world.

HUMBLENESS: the awareness of our dependence on Spirit and the awareness of our need for and interdependence with other human beings and the world around us on all levels.

IDENTIFICATION: the state of the "I" without presence when it is unconsciously absorbed in one of the functions of thought, feeling, or action.

INTELLECT: thought, distinguished from the faculties of the subconscious/superconscious mind; mind activated by will and reason; the faculty of mind most under our immediate control.

INTENTION: an aim or wish, clearly formulated in words, by which we mobilize the energy to attain our aim or wish.

INTERDEPENDENCE: the recognized need of human beings for one another in order to attain the fullness of life on all levels, from material to cosmic.

KNOWLEDGE: certainty. At least seven levels are recognized: knowing something's name; knowing through the senses; knowing about something; knowing through deeper grasp and understanding; knowing through doing; knowing through subtle, subconscious faculties; and knowing by Spirit alone.

LEADER: someone who is elevated by others in order to be of service, to whom we give love, respect, and everything necessary to get a particular job done.

LIFE: a primary attribute of Spirit.

LOVE: the electromagnetic milieu in which we exist, which exerts various forces of attraction among all that it contains; the greatest transforming power; our experience of Spirit.

MARRIAGE: the result or destination of our sexual maturing.

MEDITATION: listening within; a function of consciousness, not intellect.

MIND: not necessarily the effect of the individualized brain, but the whole field in which we exist.

MYSTICISM: a faculty peculiar to the human being, which is obvious neither to the senses nor to the intellect, but which depends on the refinement and receptivity of faculties within the whole mind.

NOTHINGNESS: the point reached by utmost subtilization. Like sugar dissolving in water, the self is not really gone, but absorbed.

PERSONALITY: learned habits of thought, feeling, and behavior; the social self. Personality can either obscure or magnify essence.

POINT OF CONTACT: the person, or anything, through whom we gain access to Spirit or our own Higher Self.

PRESENCE: the state of being consciously aware.

PROPHET: one who brings a code of living, or sacred law, to the majority. A prophet may also initiate an elite into the knowledge of Truth.

PSYCHE: the totality of the functions of the mind: senses; intellect; and the subtle, subconscious, creative, and spiritual departments of the mind.

REMEMBERING: another word for the state of Presence.

SENSING: a grounded awareness of the body through physical sensations.

SERVICE: the functional outcome of being connected to Cosmic Energy.

SOUL: individualized Spirit.

SPIRIT: the first and primary manifestation of the Essence we call God.

SUBMISSION: the bowing of the lower self, or ego, to the essential Self wherever it is found.

SUFI: one who understands Essence beyond forms. The word's root meaning is literally "pure, unadulterated."

TRUTH: the knowledge that we are integral to the Whole.

WILL: the ability to act consciously; the faculty of conscious choice, a unique attribute of the human being.

WISDOM: knowledge that comes from within through contact with Spirit.

WITNESS: any manifestation of Spirit.

WORSHIP: loving respect for a higher spiritual power; a yearning found in human beings.